The
Sergeant
Escapers

JOHN DOMINY

The
Sergeant
Escapers

LONDON

IAN ALLAN LTD

First published 1974

ISBN 0 7110 0569 9

Published by Ian Allan Ltd, Shepperton, Surrey,
and printed in the United Kingdom by
Morrison and Gibb Ltd, London and Edinburgh

This book is dedicated to the Regular NCOs of the Royal Air Force with respect and great affection.

Their unofficial motto was 'If you can't take a joke, you shouldn't have joined.'

They lived up to and died readily for their own wry philosophy.

Foreword

By Airey Neave DSO, OBE, MC, TD, MP

Though more than thirty years have passed, the spirit of the 'Kriegies' lives on. The German prisoner-of-war camps are now part of this troubled century. Why are they not forgotten? Perhaps it is because the 'Kriegies' had values of which Britain and the world will always be in need. You have only to read this genuine and moving book to realise what they were.

It is high time a tribute was paid to the NCOs of the RAF for their great record in the story of escape. They were modest men who have for too long been unnoticed. I do not know of any story of the prison camps which compares with that of George Grimson. There were of course heroes and heroines of secret escape lines in enemy-occupied territory, but Grimson operated his own route for fellow prisoners-of-war. He organised a line to the Baltic ports, complete with safe houses, to get his friends home. He recruited Poles and Germans into his organisation.

There is no one really like Grimson in the history of escape. Like all great leaders in underground war, he had his own mystique. We do not really know his fate. Perhaps this is why he inspires. The thought of his lone figure, still out there beyond the wire, will always be with those who survived. So this book is a splendid memorial to him and the NCOs of the RAF, like the author, whom we should honour today.

AIREY NEAVE

Author's Preface

This book is dated. It deals with events of 30 years ago in the terminal era of old-world thought, before the last war. I have tried to reproduce authentically, possibly for the first time, what happened in a small pocket of that era, the RAF wartime prison camp, how we really thought, what we actually said and did, though that is not the main object of writing this book, which is to record some of the fabulous escape stories from German prison camps for NCOs of the RAF. It is also to provide some memorial for the largely unnoticed NCO escapers and particularly for one of them, George Grimson, who is surely one of the great escapers of all·time. Their courage, flexibility, ingenuity and fortitude in adversity is not dated. I believe it still lies beneath the less heroic face of the British people of today waiting to be called forth by circumstances. If you are surprised at some of the attitudes evident in this book, remember that basic virtues wear many faces.

Over many years I am indebted to James Alexander Deans, MBE, RAF, 'Mr Standfast', who after his incredible service to Britain, in which his steadfastness was a byword, has borne for more than 20 years since the war a painful and distressing disease with fortitude and high courage. Much of his spare time is spent in looking after other people, including his own ex-Kriegies, to whom he is still 'King Dixie'.

My old colleague and comrade Cyril Aynsley, now OBE, recently retired after many years' service as Chief Reporter of the *Daily Express*, has made available to me a considerable amount of material which he and 'Dixie' collected with the idea of writing a book of this kind. Much of the material came from George's brother John, with whom I have not been able to make contact so many years later. I hope he and his family will accept this tribute to his brother. It comes from the hearts of many old comrades.

The self-effacing Nat Leaman has also provided a great deal of information of those brave days of long ago. So have John Heape and many others too numerous to mention. They are now to be found as far afield as Canada, New Zealand, South Africa, Rhodesia, America and Europe.

I would like to record a debt of gratitude to many others who made the twilight war of prison a worthwhile experience. The ebullient Peter Fox springs to mind, W. E. 'Sandy' Sands who took many of the pictures in this book while still 'in the bag', Jas Lambert, 'Buffy' James and 'Nobby' Clarke, all Regular RAF; Red Gordon, Ivan B. Quinn and 'The Tank' from our Canadian contingent; Stan Ablomowitz (now a new Aussie) and his Poles; 'V.R.' Nuvotny and the Czechs; Jack Garret, heading the Kiwis who included a Dam Buster; and Joe Galland.

Then come the incomparable Aussies, whose contempt for the enemy was always a great encouragement. They included men such as Mick Chisholm, who although he suffered from claustrophobia was always at the top of the escape list.

Back on the British side again were such sterling characters as Larry Slattery and Georgie Booth, Vic Clarke, Ken Griffiths, 'Ginger' Sheppherd and former all-in wrestler 'Tiny' Bushell. Now alas many are dead, but there are still enough of us to meet in England from all over the world for such occasions as the memorial service for Larry Slattery.

No book of this kind would be complete without recourse to such fine centres of information as the RAF Air Historical Branch and the RAF Museum at Henlow, where Bristow's two secret radios are still to be seen. My thanks are also due to Group Captain E. B. Haslam MA, FR, Hist. S of the RAF Air Historical Branch and Group Captain W. E. 'Bill' Randle OBE, AFC, DFM, who was himself a successful evader and who is now responsible for the RAF Museum.

Finally, there is the man who keeps us all informed, Cal Younger, with his magazine *The Kriegie*.

I have missed many who should be mentioned. I hope they will forgive me and remember that this book is mainly for George.

Prologue

The Germans used to keep a special camp coffin at Heydekrug, the prisoner of war camp for NCOs of the RAF way up on the Baltic and now part of Russia.

More than anything else, that coffin probably underlined the Nazi attitude towards us; although by the time we had finished with the *Herrenvolk*, a certain change in the Nazi mind had no doubt taken place.

All the same, the coffin was a symbol of the 'Jerry', as the British prisoner preferred to call him – the Jerry at his worst – for it was no ordinary coffin. It was collapsible and had a hinged floor. It was also very large, so that it fitted over the grave. When the bolts were drawn during the committal, the body hit the bottom of the grave with a sickening thump. Only a certain sort of German could have thought of this final insult to the dead, although in strict fairness we found the whole thing was as distasteful to many real Luftwaffe flying men, who in common with us had looked the old Grim Reaper in the face, as it was to us.

Of course, by the time the Germans got around to sending the NCOs to their special camp at Heydekrug, the British bomber offensive was really beginning to hurt. Influential Nazi party members were on the increase in relatively safe jobs, like those offered as guards in prison camps. The coffin represented that sort of German.

A number of German officers and other ranks, however, were different. They got on with us and had some measure of our respect. They were usually recovering from wounds received on one of the many fronts or were well-decorated relics of great dignity, who had served their country with distinction in the First World War.

But that coffin . . . the memory of it still sticks in my craw. Wherever we went, so too did the coffin – from Heydekrug to Thorn and then to Fallingbostel. As Greater Germany got smaller and smaller, it came with us – although during the unusually hard winter of 1944 a gentleman, subsequently to attain ministerial rank in the British Government, was discovered trying to make away with it for use as firewood.

Back to funerals, however. When the committal had finished and the bolts drawn, the burying detail – usually Poles or some other race the Nazis were trying without much success to enslave – had the job of dismantling it. After that they had to return it all washed and clean to the *Vorlager*, the German camp office and stores area, for the next funeral.

One of the touching things about funerals and indeed about our whole captivity was the courage of many Polish women who went, at great personal risk and often during the night curfew, to lay flowers on the new grave of some young British boy quite unknown to them. For this and many another debt we owe to that brave and generous people, we are grateful.

All the same that coffin job has always seemed to typify the German for us. Was he really the ruthlessly efficient, cold and insensitive Teuton of the 1914–1918 propaganda? He was certainly not always efficient or escape from a POW camp would have been impossible. The screaming, shouting pandemonium which often accompanied events deserving of no more than an off-hand discussion to the British mind was anything but cold.

I think there may be an insensitive streak in the Germans. Perhaps that is what helped condition the immense company of geniuses their race has produced. Perhaps it helped to make warmer the 'good' German with whom the camp guard was sprinkled – or the scrupulously correct, just and often sympathetic old Junker type, who must have been such an excellent officer to serve under and who was usually by no means a bad friend to the prisoner.

The true 'Kriegie' – the word comes from *Kriegsgefangener*, German for war prisoner, and was the name our POW used to call himself – had a complex way of looking at his captor. There was something of that now defunct but good old British attitude towards foreigners, an unconsciously superior if indulgent pity. It was reserved particularly for those who acted in an un-British way. There was what is now called a love-hate complex, too. The call of duty generated some hate; and tolerance and humanity, through association, created some love.

But things like the coffin, and in particular enthusiastic Nazis, were difficult to stomach. It is easy to imagine how and where many little Hitlers might appear in contemporary Britain if the political situation favoured them. It was not so easy for the young RAF man of the early war years to understand the type. He had not perhaps looked deeply into the psychology of even his own race then. None of us had then lost an Empire. What is more, the Germans had had about ten successful years of intensive training in becoming the *Herrenvolk* of the world by the time most of us were shot down. That had not suited the German temperament. Apart from its tendency to throw up into authority some bad thugs, the Nazi ethos seemed to underline and encourage German weaknesses – that streak of insensitivity, desire for mastery and tenacity of purpose (or was it ruthlessness?). The result, to us at any rate, did not seem at all pretty in those days.

It has been the fashion since the war for a lot of people whose necks we helped to save to decry the bombing of Germany and to forget the sacrifices made by our Service. Well, let me say here and now that I am proud to have been a *Luftgangster*, as the natives used to call us. It is difficult still to feel too sorry for the Jerries in this respect. They couldn't take the joke when it was turned against them.

Inside the prison camp, the RAF inmates made a joke of the coffin. It was known as the 'way out' or, by the ever-cheerful Gerry Tipping who was shot down in 1940, as 'the hole in the elephant's bottom'. Gerry came from Lytham St Annes in Lancashire and it was only years later I learned the full meaning of the expression when I heard that great Lancashire folk-song of the same title.

It was a final way out of captivity. But not the only way, as George Grimson and his valiant band – Alan Morris, Nat Leaman, Paddy Flockhart, Jock Alexander, 'Aussie' Lascelles, 'Wimpy' Wootton, 'Nobby' Clarke and a host of other unknown and certainly unsung characters – were to prove.

George was the epitome of an escaper among the NCOs, as Squadron Leader Roger Bushell and Lieutenant Commander Jimmy Buckley RN were among the officers. George was also one of the many who has not returned.

He did not disappear through the famous hole. After making some of the most original and exciting escapes on record, he went out to establish an underground escape route through Lithuania, Poland and East Prussia, with safe houses where a prisoner might stay and recuperate for the final attempt to get out of Germany. It was a route along which he sent only others to freedom. His own fate is still a mystery, though officially he has been certified dead. After trying to rescue one of his comrades, picked up by the dock guards at Danzig, he was probably taken by the Gestapo. In that case it is likely that his high concept of duty, self-imposed, brought him to torture and the final end. Somewhere near Insterburg his ashes or his bones may now hallow some small spot in what is today supposed to be Free Poland.

When we returned after the war, Grimson was recommended for the VC by those who had known him. At that time the Air Ministry officials could not establish his death. It was some years before this was even officially assumed and every one knows how important that sort of thing is to the civil servant. However, some years after his death had been registered at Whitehall, a serving officer who had been a successful evader wrote yet another recommendation for a high posthumous award. Still nothing was done. To us George was a legend; to civil servants he seems to have been just an awkward name that had a habit of cropping up again and again. Rather a nuisance really! 'If you can't take a joke . . .'

The war was over and so were the days of the wartime aircrew.

Boisterous and devoted doers of the job in hand were out of fashion. A brave new world was dawning under Attlee. There was an abundance of people appearing from beneath safe stones, all busy telling us what to do. Their main interest seemed to be personal survival and increasing the empire of their own species. George was a nasty reminder of other things – great things like courage and sacrifice for one's country or one's comrades. What better than to try and sweep his memory under the carpet or better still pretend it had never happened. But it did happen. Some of the men who had carried on the twilight war of the escaper came back – at least enough of them to tell the story.

Finally let it be said that thirty members of His Majesty's Air Forces escaped from German prison camps and got home. Sixteen of them were NCOs. This is the story of some of them in general and of George Grimson in particular. It seems likely to be his only memorial.

Chapter 1

THE setting of this tale is essentially a grim one – the prison camps of Germany where we were only protected from the worst aspects of Nazi savagery by the Geneva Convention and the innate decency of some of the German Luftwaffe officers, who did their best to behave in a manner befitting their service and their religion. (Incidentally, many of the best men were Prussians; some of the real bastards came from 'nice' holiday places like Bavaria.) To make matters worse, the good Germans were themselves liable to fall victims of a denunciation by Gestapo or Party members who riddled the lower ranks of the camp guards.

All camps, except the fortress or castle prisons like Thorn and Colditz, were built on much the same lines. In fact, there was little difference in construction between them and the concentration camps. Rows of huts or single-storey buildings huddled in a surround of lots of wire, dotted with guard boxes each sheltering a bored and sometimes murderous guard. He had a machine gun as well as a swivelling light to search the compounds after dark. These camps were strictly utility jobs, no doubt the design of a German civil servant – one of Speer's pupils perhaps! In the view of the increasingly bloody-minded inmates, whoever was responsible had without a doubt received a high Party award – 'crossed lips for backside licking' was Ron West's suggestion.

The prisons were all 'especially designed escape-proof camps' created for the 'black prisoners'. The Germans graded their prisoners black, white and grey, depending upon their attempts to escape or create a nuisance. Aircrew were automatically black: and none blacker than us, for whom they had to create a special *Lager* in the centre of the great complex of prison *Lager* in Stalag VIIIb, Lamsdorf, Silesia.

But the chap who designed these 'escape-proof' places was about as successful as that group of people who formed a committee not long ago with the aim of working out an escape-proof British prison. It is notable that the latter came up with the solution of a 'high security' area rather than an escape-proof prison. (It is also worth comment that they did not see fit to include among the impressive names of the committee that of a single escaper from the Second World War; there were plenty available and men like 'Wings' Day, Jimmy Deans or Jock Alexander could certainly

have given the committee and the Prison Service something to think about.)
Escape-proof prisons do not exist – not while there are men with the will
to escape.

A factor in our favour was that we were not felons or professional crooks.
We were proud members of the Force which had saved Britain and was
now doing Germany a lot of mischief. We were of course the objects of
plenty of hatred from the German politicians who inspired the posters
calling us *Terrorflieger*, *Luftgangster* or even worse. So there was not much
future for the non-German speaker on the run in Germany unless he was
exceptionally fortunate.

For us inside there was always the wire. It cut across thought, mind and
vision like a bright scar – a constant reminder that we were there at the
unpredictable mercy of *those* people.

Not that there wasn't plenty of humour despite this; for who could
restrain the spirits of the best of Britain and the Empire's youth, especially
when dealing with the thicker specimens of the native?

In fact the Germans were to supply a great deal of the humour. There
was for instance the *Abwehr* (security) officer who, over-confident of his
command of the English language, had a notice displayed: 'If you touch
the warning wire, it will be shot'; or the incredible announcement made
by another *Abwehr* officer: "You think I know f—— nothing. Let me tell
you I know f—— all."

Better still was the time when the helpful German 'goon' (Kriegie slang
for security man) leapt over the warning wire to fetch a football we had
kicked there. He was shot by an over-zealous sentry. That was at Heydekrug and anything was good for a laugh there. This particular effort had
us in fits.

But there was always the wire in whichever camp they moved us to:
Luft I in Pomerania; Luft III in Silesia; or Luft VI, the final NCOs' camp
at Heydekrug, north of Memel – "where", as Stan Shirley was heard to
comment, "we're so bloody close to Russia that when the wind's from
the east you can hear the droskies howl."

To Heydekrug came many of our comrades from various Army camps,
until we were one great big, and from the Jerry point of view, unlovable
lot. In passing one should mention that it became the thing to boast about
the tough camps. To have belonged to tough Lamsdorf had a cachet rather
like being an old Etonian.

As I have already mentioned, the pattern of each camp was much the
same architecturally, and of course the wire was the same. The inside of
each compound was surrounded by a waist-high strand of it. Fifty metres
distant was the main wire, composed of a fence of squares of barbed wire
eleven feet high, with a similar fence running parallel about six feet away.
The space between the two squared wire fences was filled with rolls and

rolls of danert wire. A pretty tough proposition to go through or over! But men did it – and some lived.

In the fifty-metre area between warning wire and main wire was the killing ground. Any prisoner found there was fair game for the guards, some of whom were only too anxious to earn a week's leave by despatching him.

Even that was not the end of it. Beyond the compounds was the *Vorlager*, also contained with a single barbed wire wall. Here lay, besides the administrative offices, the barracks of the enemy. There was also a small primitively supplied hospital, which until later in the war housed only medical NCOs, of whom we had one, and volunteers who took medical status. Perhaps the greatest thing that happened to us at Heydekrug was the arrival of two real British Army doctors, the splendid Forrest-Hay and the ever-cheerful Paddy Pollock. If the Royal Army Medical Corps has a special roll for men of fortitude and courage, those two names should be high upon it.

Finally, and perhaps the most important place in the *Vorlager*, there was the 'cooler'. This was the cell block where delinquents, according to the German book of rules, suffered hard arrest. For NCOs this meant bread and water with a proper meal every third day according to the Geneva Convention. Sometimes that old Convention was forgotten, for the Germans had extraordinary lapses of memory. But in general it was observed.

Certainly at Sagan, where Tony Hunter spent a great deal of time in the cooler, he had it 'organised' so that everyone got a reasonable hot meal every day. Hunter preparing for the 'quod' was an impressive sight, with cigarettes tied in his crotch and his bedding bulging with contraband food and writing material – for he was seriously writing verse and has since become a writer of some note.

Then there was our attitude towards the enemy. We would not wear caps because under that Convention we were required to salute an enemy of any rank; we therefore contented ourselves with an eyes right or left to German officers only. One of the reasons Tony Hunter got so much 'bird', incidentally, was his failure to salute anybody. This used particularly to annoy one *Oberzehlmeister* (Quartermaster), who would wait for Tony and get him every time, until we complained of victimisation to the Protecting Power.

But perhaps our attitude stemmed from the early days when the camp at Barth was filled largely with Regular Air Force NCOs, and only a sprinkling of Auxiliaries and VRs (Volunteer Reservists). I think it was Chiefy, later WO, Taylor-Gill who remarked there to the splendid Bertie Le-Voi that "the bloody squareheads are just another lot of natives". The two of them also referred to our compound and its quarters as 'the cantonment'. This had a fine Imperial ring about it. Both characters had served overseas in what was then the Empire, wore bushy cavalry moustaches and were always immaculately turned out. "Must put on a good show to inspect the natives", summed up Bertie one day, as we were being herded out for one of the two daily *Appells* or countings.

For many of the VRs like myself and later new boys, this was morale-uplifting. Certainly these men and others like them – for instance, the late Larry Slattery and 'Wee Georgie' Booth, the tough little Yorkshire and RAF boxer, who argued between them the distinction of being No. 1 prisoner of the Royal Air Force – would have been a tonic at any time, good or bad; and there were often bad times.

We were a mixed lot, especially as 'Butch' Harris's bomber offensive began to bite home and casualties grew. Although we were nominally all of the same rank, there was a sort of hierarchy which grew up from the time you were shot down. The newly shot down remained 'sprogs' until some newer prisoners came in to take their place. It was a bit like school all over again.

Top of the table, as it were, came Larry Slattery and Georgie Booth. Taylor-Gill, often known as TG, had been shot down on a photo-reconnaissance way back in early 1940. Then there were victims of the Chamberlain paper war, whose job had been to drop leaflets, but not to bomb: or to bomb only towards the sea! Rather like the survivors of the Light Brigade were the men who had made up our Air Force in France, and who had finished their flying on targets like the Maastricht Bridges, which should have been blown but weren't. They included characters like Bertie Le-Voi, the redoubtable Pepper, 'Wink' Winkler (who could pass a threaded needle through the skin of his leg) and 'Doc' Hastie who was to introduce many of us to the delights of that great bard Macgonagall. And there was, of course, a quiet man named George Grimson.

When you first fell into their hands, the usual greeting from the Germans was rather an oily one. "For you the war is over. There is nothing to do but wait." A tacit suggestion that you were going to sag back and laze until one side or the other won. So far as the Royal Air Force were concerned, the Jerries came considerably unstuck in this assumption.

In the beginning most people wanted desperately to get away, but had no knowledge of the techniques of escape. And after going through, under or over the wire, what then? It was a long way back to England. But there were always the five per cent, the dedicated, completely determined escapers – men like George Grimson.

It took everyone some time to realise that escape was a military operation. Like all such operations it had to be meticulously planned; it also had to have a firm base, which meant the hundred per cent support of everyone in the camp. That this came about was due to a number of things.

First I would place the utter dedication of George Grimson, Alan Morris and the hard-core escapers. Alongside this must stand the incredible leadership of James Alexander Graham Deans, MBE, who took over and organised the entire camp life, and risked his own neck on a number of occasions. And then there was John Bristow, the delightful and inventive extrovert who built radios from mess-tins and any odds and ends which he could lay his hands on. 'Curly' Bristow, so-called because of his crop of tight fair curls, supplied that other essential ingredient for a military force, the morale-lifter, the link with home – the secret wireless, codeword 'Canary'.

Jimmy Deans' hold over the whole organisation ensured that the BBC news was taken verbatim by *Daily Express* reporters Ron Mogg and Cyril Aynsley practically every night for four years and disseminated by specially selected 'readers'. Their job was to present the news in the unemotional accents of the BBC of those days. This was important; for a statement, particularly one from Churchill, was likely to be mulled over and discussed ad infinitum. Everything came to be controlled and had behind it the shrewd and dedicated personality of James Deans.

This was the eventual organisation which was to back George Grimson and his associates, not only in planning and making some of the most daring escapes in war prison history, but also in helping to build up the escape route through enemy country from Heydekrug to Danzig.

After all the effort and dedication, the success story may sound small. Two NCOs got back to England along the Grimson route. Others like Townsend-Coles were caught by the Gestapo and killed. But they had won their victory. They had shown the Germans how slight was their hold upon us. They had involved large numbers of the German Army and other organisations, such as the Hitler *Jugend*, or Youth Organisations, in searching for them. Time, fuel, machines and men had all been taken from the real job of fighting. What is more, Grimson had by then shaken the German security organisation to the core by showing how it could be infiltrated and outwitted. Every man of the Royal Air Force should be proud of the record of its prisoners and remember the men who were responsible.

In two books written recently much is made of a supposed rift between NCOs and officers. Of course neither of the authors of these books were with us. Probably they hadn't been born then. They certainly did not have 'a number', which was the criterion for our exclusive comradeship.

Among the fighting aircrews there was a comradeship which did not take rank into consideration. This comradeship went with us into prison camp. In the initial years, until the NCOs were segregated at Heydekrug, our cage was always close to that of the officers. We were frequently their concern and it was they who made over a portion of their pay to create a fund for the otherwise penniless NCOs. This was to have a tremendous effect on the camp and was a means of gaining essential escape aids.

Apart from that, who could live in the next compound to men like 'Wings' Day, Squadron Leader Roger Bushell and Lt Commander James Buckley, RN, without catching something of their magic spirit?

"Organise, organise," said James Buckley when he got the chance to speak to people in our compound. "Organise and then escape." "To escape is your duty," preached Day. "Every successful escape is a victory for your country."

James Buckley lived and died by his own code. He was found drowned after, it is believed, an attempt to cross from Denmark to Sweden by canoe. Roger Bushell was killed by the Germans. 'Wings' is still with us.

None of our officers let us down. I hope they feel the same about us.

The snag was that to the Germans anyone without a commission was worm-high. Amazingly this too seemed to be the view of the Geneva Convention, which permitted officers to receive part of their pay. NCOs officially received nothing, so that we could only hope for a parcel from home or from the Red Cross to supplement our wants.

Our officers saw to it that we had money. It is typical of the attitude of a peace-time Air Ministry that the return of this money to the survivors, who so readily subscribed it, had to be the subject of a long wrangle when we returned. Like the officers, all prisoners of war also paid income tax for the delights of being lousy and hungry in Germany. But, of course, so too did the poor devil living in a hole in the desert or fighting through the monsoon in Burma. There is nothing like paying for your pleasures!

In the NCOs' camp, as in the officers', the mixture of Regular, Auxiliary, VR and 'Hostilities Only' took a little time to settle down. But when the mixture got going it was trouble for the Germans all the way round. On their side they seemed to think this was all wrong. To the Germans a prisoner was a prisoner. Their view was that this was quite an honourable estate and a fate which could befall anyone in battle. From their point of view we were truculent, unco-operative, un-soldierly and ill-disciplined. I suppose we must have been a bit trying to these rather earnest characters who just wanted a quiet life.

It was a bit of a bind for us too. We had landed up in a place where, foreign to the training of any of us, our captors actually abused and struck their own men of lower rank in front of us. This was disgraceful. Especially as the German junior officers were not immune from such treatment.

On one occasion at Heydekrug, an elderly, wall-eyed professor of Bonn, who had become popular with us because he treated us like human beings and was so old that he attracted the nickname of 'Jiminy Cricket', was actually bawled out in front of us by the Commandant. The reaction was immediate. The Commandant was booed and jeered until he finally stalked off the parade ground in an impotent huff. Even the Germans had a sense of humour, of a kind; a rebuff like this was known to them as 'being given a cigar'.

As part of our general bloody-mindedness, we objected to being referred to as soldiers, which was the common method of address for members of the Luftwaffe. From time to time we explained that we were airmen, *not* 'Brown Jobs'. It took a long time for this to get through to the Jerry mind, but at least they were in hearty agreement we were *not* soldiers. Perhaps they had something there.

There was one word guaranteed to get the Germans really going, and that was 'Hun'. Although you could point out that it was a perfectly good word with an entry in the English dictionary, it was a sure passport to the cooler amid a frenzy of shouting and arm waving.

To us most of the Germans seemed to have inordinately loud voices and to enjoy using them at full throttle. Every civilian seemed to wear some sort of fancy uniform too, and anyone with a brown shirt acted as if he were the Führer himself (but there are people in England, particularly in the bureaucracy, who are a bit like that too, unless they are sharply brought to heel). We used to feel a little puzzled. From the Germans we encountered it was difficult to remember that this was a race which had produced some of the world's great philosophers, composers, poets and scientists – though most of them were dead and their works proscribed or else they had been driven out of their country by the Nazis, who used to have such fun burning books.

Prisoners we might be, but the teaching of 'Wings' Day, Roger Bushell and Jimmy Buckley, backed by the unshakeable faith of our NCO Regulars, began to grip the whole camp. Even as prisoners there was glory to be won, still much fighting to be faced.

Chapter 2

TO those who failed to notice his Viking eyes, George Grimson might have seemed rather ordinary. He was slimly built and got even slimmer as escape, recapture and sentences on bread and water in solitary confinement fined him down. His medium height belied his considerable strength. His brown hair, which turned more and more to grey, might have persuaded the unobservant to write him off as ageing. But the eyes showed that behind that ordinary, straightforward, if somewhat uncommunicative, façade there was a wealth of fortitude, courage and resource. He was to need all of it in the months ahead.

A typical story of the youthful George is told by his brother John, to whom he was greatly attached.

"We were living at Putney, and because we were so close to the Thames we used to spend much of our time on the banks of the river. George was eighteen, pretty tough and wiry, but he got me worried one day.

"It was a normal sort of day for us, but somehow or other a quarrel arose with some other boys who were on the river bank. I could see George was angry and also that a fight was likely to develop. I just couldn't understand it when George suddenly turned to me, said 'I'm going' and promptly took to his heels. I just couldn't believe it; but I carried on with the quarrel alone.

"Ten minutes later George was back again, a little breathless, but in spite of that he waded into his opponent, knocked him into the water and then jumped in after him. Soon it was all over; the bully jumped out and ran away.

" 'You had me worried,' I said to George as we squelched our watery way home to Putney, 'When you ran away like that, I thought you'd gone yellow.' George laughed. 'I was wearing my best suit,' he explained, 'so I just nipped off home and changed before getting stuck in.' "

This rather off-hand way of surprising achievement was all George. It was one of his great qualities which endeared him to his family and was to earn him many friends in hard places in the times of adversity.

Pretty well everything that George did was well thought out, simple and direct. His reasons for becoming Regular aircrew in 1938 when he was twenty-two illustrate this. A year or so earlier, an older brother, one of four, had died after an accident at work. George's father, deeply affected by the tragedy, died soon after. At the time George was studying to be an architect. There was no welfare state in those days and special education grants were few and far between. It was typical of George that he should decide that it was his duty to go out to work and help his widowed mother. This was at a time when Britain was just emerging from the greatest depression in history and jobs were still hard to get. In the building trade all that the Labour Exchange could offer was work as a labourer. The work was hard. With bleeding fingers George stuck it out until one of his hands became infected and he was laid off work.

While he convalesced he thought over the whole problem and quietly made his decision. "I am going to the Air Ministry in Kingsway to see if I can join up," he told his mother. "But all your studies," said his mother. "you'll just be throwing it all away!" "Don't worry," replied George. "I'll make the RAF my career instead."

At Uxbridge George cheerfully did his square-bashing on the parade ground. He moaned at the usual things the airmen, or 'plonks' moaned at, drank the NAAFI tea and ate the sparsely buttered 'wads' of bread, and absorbed the Service into his being. Soon he was doing aircrew training as a wireless-operator-airgunner. He was also boxing for his unit and duly won a medal in a lightweight competition. He came home proudly wearing his flying brevet and gave his boxing medal to his mother. "Here you are," he said. "It cost me six fights and two black eyes, so take care of it."

It was the only medal George was going to get.

War came and George was in an operational squadron. He spoke little of this at home and his mother only knew that he was flying over enemy territory from a chance remark he had made to his friends. In fact he was flying in that splendid creation of Barnes Wallis, the Wellington bomber, known affectionately throughout the RAF as the 'Wimpy'. Even the Germans knew it by this name. Their interrogators often referred to the 'Vickers Vellington Vimpy'. To George and to many other members of the Service, it was the finest aircraft of its time. Although the Mark ic in which he was flying was greatly underpowered, it bore for many years the heat and turmoil of the battle in the skies all over the world.

Like so many of the early hands, George and his crew did their share of pamphlet dropping, bombing 'only towards the sea' and all the other stupid little restricted operations of Chamberlain's war. But at last the Phoney War ended and 37 Squadron with the rest of the RAF was in the thick of it. While Fighter Command hacked the skies over England clear of Göring's men, other Commands of the Service had their part to play. As the Army reeled back from Dunkirk, farsighted men prepared for a possible battle of England. Bomber and Coastal Commands, with the heroic Fleet Air Arm men in their out-of-date 'Stringbags', got busy; 'bashing the barges' and 'knocking the docks' became the order of the day and night. Meanwhile the German Army started to prepare for invasion and the Battle of Britain.

On the evening of 14th July 1940, George and his crew made their way across the airfield to aircraft L for Luv. It was the usual sort of start to a raid. Briefing had been carried out earlier. The target was the dockyards of the German port of Hamburg, where barges were already being assembled.

A last look round, a moment of listening to late bird song and of drawing in the sweet smell of the English countryside, then the first aircraft shattered the evening quiet as the Pegasus engines started their warm-up run. A quick look round and George was up into L for Luv, closing the hatch behind him and then taking his place at the radio, already checked on the morning's 'Night Flying Test'.

Meantime the pilot went through his cockpit drill with his 'second dicky', and front and rear gunners eased back the cocking-studs on their twin Brownings. "OK. Let's go", came the captain's voice on the R/T.

Like a clumsy bird Wimpy L for Luv waddled around the perimeter track to take-off position. One more run-up of the engines, a magneto and oil pressure check, and the pilot signalled the control tower that he was ready. A green light flashed from the tower. The Wimpy started on its take-off run as the captain increased power on the engines and adjusted the pitch of his airscrews. In a torrent of noise, the bomb-laden aircraft lifted easily, wheels retracted and the ungainly bird of the ground became as graceful as a hawk in flight.

A left-hand circuit of the airfield, gaining height (the Germans did alternate right- and left-hand circuits), and the plane was back over the airfield to enable the observer to get a good departure point for navigation. Now they were on their way eastwards. A most mundane sort of war this, with most of the crew thinking of eggs and bacon in the mess when they got back.

The Wimpy was not a fast aircraft by the time that the Air Ministry had modified the original Barnes Wallis design. With radio silence imposed on the way out, there was little for George to do except take the occasional radio D/F fix and hand it to the observer, who in those days did everything from bomb aiming to navigation and spare gunner.

There was the usual dusting of flak over the enemy coast and, with Oldenburg away to starboard, the aircraft slid steadily on to Hamburg, where searchlights and flak burst could already be seen in the sky. The observer made his way to the bomb-aimer's position and set his estimated wind and drift on the course setting of the bomb-sight. Then he selected his bombs and started to talk the pilot on the run-in. Underneath and around them the flak raged, starkly visible, for the Germans went in for a lot of coloured ammunition which could be rather off-putting until one became used to it.

In his radio position, ready to take over a gun if one of the gunners was hit, George heard the calm exchanges between observer and pilot.

"Left a little."

The aircraft veered.

"Steady. Bombing run-up starting."

The observer took the small push switch, familiarly known as the 'tit', in his hand.

"Bomb doors open."

"Doors open. Stand by."

"Right a little."

"Check. Spot on! Keep this course."

The target crept along the sighting wires to the release position. The observer pressed 'the tit' and the aircraft, relieved of the weight of its bombs, rose in the air.

"Bombs gone, close bomb doors."

"Bomb doors closed."

The flak was getting fiercer.

"For Christ's sake, lets get out of this lot," said the pilot on the R/T.

"Steer two-ninety," said the observer, returning to his navigation duties. The aircraft banked gracefully to the left into a salvo of flak. There was a thump and the sour smell of cordite.

Within minutes the aircraft's course, in spite of the damage, had brought it over the Bremen flak defences. The pilot turned southwards again, seeking another route to the sea. But a burst in the wing was followed by a neat bracket of four. They made a noise like a sharp cough when they were near you. Wimpy L for Luv was on fire.

Holding the aircraft as straight and level as he could, the captain gave the triple "Jump, Jump, Jump!" order. Encumbered by his 'Mae West' life-jacket and his chest position parachute, George stood on the mainspar, released the astrodome and pushed his way out into the howling slipstream.

The aircraft slid past. Then he felt a sudden jerk and heard the soft rustle of silk as his parachute developed. He looked down at his gloved right hand and noticed that it still held the D release ring which he could not remember pulling. For a moment or two he swung in the soft night air and then hit the ground. He had just about made it by seconds. Nearby his aircraft lit the sky as it blew up.

In those days few aircrew were prepared for escape, especially from inside Germany. But in any case there were Germans abounding where George came down. His captors seemed pleased with themselves. There would have been less pleasure had they known who the night wind had dropped on to German soil. George Grimson was down, unhurt: and, to quote a friend, 'bloody annoyed'.

Back in England George's mother had, as so many other wartime mothers, 'a premonition that something had gone wrong and something had happened to George'. It was a Sunday and to cheer herself up she went to the pictures, but the premonition grew stronger. On Monday she heard on the BBC the words 'Two of our aircraft are missing . . .' A little later came the cold, confirmatory telegram from the Air Ministry. Later still she was to learn from a squadron friend that George had managed to bale out and was unhurt, although a prisoner of war, in what Ronnie West was later to describe as the 'Third and Last Reich'.

At Dulag Luft, the reception centre for Air Force prisoners at Oberursel near Frankfurt-am-Main, George stayed briefly and was singularly unhelpful to the interrogators. As one might have expected, his first card home to his brother John was brief and very much to the point. "Sorry to upset the family," he wrote, "but it could not be helped. This war gets in the way but I was comparatively lucky. Look after Mother for me and don't get mixed up in too many fights. One of us in the cooler at one time is enough. The best of luck. Your brother George." As a postscript he added: "Keep your eye on the Duce." George might be in prison but he was far from subdued. Nor had he lost his concern for other people.

His prison number had now been allotted. It was *Kriegsgefangener* No 134, an early one which put him among the 'quality' – the first of the many to be shot down for England to taste the bitter delights of Nazi hospitality.

When enough Air Force and Fleet Air Arm prisoners had been collected to form what the Jerries called 'a transport', George like so many others was sent to Stalag Luft 1, at Barth, Vogelsand, in what was then Pomerania.

That such an unpleasant place should have had such a nice name – 'bird beach' – seemed appropriate in *our* Germany. The town of Barth, which lies in the Zingst Haff, a large inlet sheltered from the Baltic by the sandy, forested arm of the Zingst Peninsula, was dominated by a gigantic, ugly square-built church with a great, thick spire. To the south and east of the view from the camp it overpowered the eye. Like the barbed wire, it was menacing and large. It was the very bully of a church. Nor, as he got to know the Germans better, was George surprised to find that the camp was next to a military target, a German anti-aircraft regimental school for recruits to the German Army. This was, of course, in direct contravention of the Geneva Convention.

Generally speaking, though, the Germans behaved themselves reasonably at this period, for they were on the crest of their winning wave. The journey to Barth was actually made in third-class rail compartments – accompanied by guards, of course.

It was from one of these 'transports' that a sergeant was later to detach himself and, although dressed in RAF uniform and flying boots, to wander around the goods yard at Frankfurt until he found a horse-drawn dray. He felt it was just as well he had, for noises in the other part of the goods yard, where prisoners were entraining, indicated that his absence had been discovered. Whistles were shrilling through the shouts and yells that accompanied so much the Germans did.

It was time to go. Quickly the prisoner leapt into the driver's seat, picked up the reins and loudly cried "Gee up" in English.

The horses remained perfectly still and the guards came round the corner. Hands up, the prisoner had to get down. The German driver of the dray now turned up, wiping his lips from the quiet beer he had been having, to be soundly rated by the *Feldwebel*. He spat, climbed on to his box, shook the reins and grunted "Gurrr". Whereat the horses moved off briskly and the prisoner was hustled back to the party.

As the escaper, who was to become one of the most irrepressible characters in Kriegiedom, was dragged and pushed into the train, he remarked sadly: "What a bloody country. Even the horses can only speak German."

Chapter 3

BARTH was a bad camp, though not so much from the point of view of the accommodation, which even for NCOs was quite reasonable. Many of the first lessons in the war of escape were learned here – by both sides. At Barth we were in the hands of the Luftwaffe, and with a few exceptions, correct military treatment was the order of the day. It might have been harsh, but little attempt was made to rob prisoners of their pride in their Service or of their own manhood.

Soon after George arrived, the NCO prisoners were most unexpectedly asked if they would like to help gather in the harvest. Even the Germans should have been bright enough to realise that an almost one hundred per cent response to this offer invited suspicion. But they were under the impression that the British had decided the war was as good as over and were going to settle down and become 'good boys', as the commandant was so fond of suggesting.

What is more, the rations for prisoners working on farms arrived in bulk and were issued in bulk every fourteen days. This was vital, because it was a long time before Red Cross parcels or personal parcels reached Barth; prisoners had no stocks of easily portable food so essential for escape. Of course, there had been too little time to set up any organisation for forging passports or getting civilian clothing, or even making maps. Also few of the would-be escapers at that time had troubled to learn what they described as that "rather funny language".

All the same, ration day arrived. The prisoners, who were by now fit and comparatively well-fed from stolen eggs and the odd chicken here and there, were dished out with their rations.

Next morning the whole of Pomerania erupted in something like panic. The army was turned out, the *Jugend* was turned out. Party members and police and all the voluntary organisations scoured the hedges and ditches. Honest *Frauen* locked their doors for the first time.

They need hardly have bothered. Quite unprepared for escape, most of the prisoners were rounded up in a few hours and all were finally returned to the camp for the 'statutory' week on bread and water in the cooler. They were then posted to the 'safe' prison at Lamsdorf, Stalag VIIIb.

Strangely enough, limited parties were still permitted to harvest, and it was on one of these that George Grimson made his first break. It was an amateurish affair. He simply kicked his guard good and hard in the backside and made off. His recapture was inevitable. "Still," he remarked at the time, "I thought I'd try my luck." Duly brought back to camp, he was lodged in the cooler for a week and came out thinner, a little greyer and a good deal more thoughtful.

Cells are great places for working things out and George in his straightforward way had done some heavy thinking. "This escape lark needs a lot more going into," he said. Now twenty-four years old, he settled down to learn German.

At Barth, work parties were greatly cut down, but the need for intelligence on what was happening outside the wire had been recognised. The *Arbeiter* (worker) now went out, not to escape, but to look around, observe and prepare for better organised escapes.

'Aussie' Lascelles and his team were planning to get out by stealing a boat and sailing to Sweden in the spring. They worked in the fish-canning factory and the things they put in with the fish were to make more than one ex-Kriegie confirmed non-eaters of any canned fish.

Christmas was not a very merry one at Barth in that year of 1940. Red Cross parcels were still coming through only in dribs and drabs. Christmas dinner in the main mess hall consisted of one small piece of boiled pork, a spoonful of Sauerkraut and three potatoes. But a Christmas pantomime was played to an appreciative if somewhat intoxicated audience who, through the fund collected in the officers' camp, were able to buy beer and wine. The fact that the actors were also a little boozed helped the thing along merrily.

A few nights later Sergeant Johnnie Shaw, with another escaper, dressed in white camouflage made from sheets stolen from the hospital, attempted to crawl through the snow and cut the wire. He was spotted, challenged by the sentry and told to stand up. His companion still lay hidden in the snow. Johnnie stood up with his hands raised. The sentry took careful aim over a distance of a few yards and Johnnie fell, shot through the heart.

When the body was examined it was noticed that his coat, which was open, was untouched by the bullet, proving he was standing, unarmed, with his hands up. The marksman got some leave and no notice was taken of our protests; but we were allowed to have Johnnie laid in the small room at the end of the mess block. He had been laid out with care by the town undertaker. And he had been shaved. Perhaps the small Hitler-type moustache which was left on what was normally a clean-shaven face was an accident – or was it deliberate? A few of us would like to ask that man ourselves one day.

Of course Johnnie got a full military funeral attended by some of his comrades and representatives of the officers' compound. The Luftwaffe provided an escort and a firing party. This time they fired blanks.

At Lamsdorf, where most of the old BEF was in prison, exchanges were being made between the RAF in the centre *Lager* or camp and the soldiers in the other *Lager*. This permitted more frequent attempts to escape, as the soldiers were allowed out on working parties and here the RAF were not. It was easier to go that way than through or under the wire. But quite apart from that, the RAF were causing the 'Green Jobs' – ie the German Army, who wore green uniform – more than a little trouble, so it was decided to do a purge in reverse. Back to Barth came Grimson, Bertie Le-Voi, Wink and sundry other people who were intent upon the dissolution of the old 'Third and Last'.

In May 1941, Flight Lieutenant H. Burton, DSC, MBE, made the first successful challenge to the enemy by escaping from Barth to Sweden. It was a big boost for morale, battered due to the lack of parcels and Red Cross food. In the end, Red Cross food was the only thing that kept us going. Even if we did complain about the quality and large gap of nothing in one manufacturer's meat rolls, we were grateful.

Tunnels were all the rage. After Burton's getaway they had started to sprout in all outward directions from both NCOs' and officers' compounds.

On the German side a new menace had arrived, albeit a reasonably pleasant one. He was full of jokes and his name was *Hauptmann* Buckweig. He was the kind of enemy worth having, for although he had a dirty job to do, he did it as pleasantly and politely as he could. His story was that he was really a Croat and only serving in the Luftwaffe because he was forced to do so. In fact he disliked the Germans intensely, he said. It was a good story which no one believed.

Buckwieg was fond of illustrating the shortcomings of Germany's Italian allies to whom, like us, he referred as the "Vops" or just "Eyties". His party trick was to put his cap on back to front and then march backwards. "Look! Vops advancing," he would cry.

He also installed microphones at a number of places in the compound, particularly in the library. He must have been a little astonished one night when Paddy Flynn discovered one and hailed him down the microphone with a cry of "Bollocks, you squarehead bastard." Paddy's rich Irish accent should have made him a fair cop, but nothing was done. After that we searched for more, but when they were found we left them and issued warnings, marking them. We were learning to be more subtle. Eventually, what with us thinking up false stories, known as 'duff gen', and leaking them down the mikes, and the Germans hurrying to dig in all sorts of unlikely places, a kind of belligerent happiness pervaded both sides of the wire.

But Buckwieg had also had seismographs installed in the wire. He had an almost English sense of humour. When the hundredth tunnel was discovered and closed, Buckwieg had a large wooden tombstone recording the fact that it was the hundredth abortive attempt planted in the early hours. It was there for us all to see when we came out for the morning parade. Buckwieg contented himself with just discovering tunnels, so that when he struck it was usually at night when the tunnelling party was safely tucked up in their little two-tier wooden beds. He was not so keen as many of our guardians were on putting men in the cooler. He did his duty, but did not make a meal of his victims.

George, on whom the Germans were keeping a special eye as his exploits at Lamsdorf had made him a marked man, lived an outwardly exemplary life as far as they were concerned. But his influence was already beginning to exert itself on the more placid members of the community behind the wire. He might not appear to be involved, but his hand could be detected behind many of the attempts to escape, even though they failed in the main object, to get home.

One of the most imaginative escapes that year was the affair of the late Tubby Dixon, onetime BBC producer. The Germans had been laying surface drains in the camp and Tubby decided to take advantage of this. He organised his own working party to build a drain right through the forbidden area and on through the wire.

The working party was under the charge of George, who dressed in a pair of pyjamas dyed to look like German overalls. His belt was an ordinary leather one which had been scrounged on a working party, but his cardboard, highly-polished holster and the wooden pistol it contained were works of Kriegie art. We were learning.

The working party of prisoners was formed up. George marched us to the wire with our shovels and shouted at the guards in their machine gun-armed watch towers along the fence. They kept a bored eye on us for a time, but were then attracted at various diversions – free fights, loud arguments and the like – which had been started close to them in the compound. The working party was now joined by a German civilian (Tubby Dixon in disguise), who took a spade from one of the prisoners and dug the last few feet under the wire before squeezing through and walking down along the path beside the outer wire.

At this moment whistles in the camp summoned a snap roll call. The working party hurried off to get into place and to cover up for Tubby. A correct count was made – the cover-up system had begun to work perfectly – but Tubby was not away. At the foot of the path he encountered a smiling Buckwieg, who unusually did not trouble to draw his pistol.

"My commiserations, Mr Dixon," he said, extending his hand. "You deserved to escape and I would like to have seen you succeed. The only trouble is, if you escape I lose my job and they might even put me in prison in a castle. They do that to German officers, you know. Allow me to escort you to the cooler."

On their way, the *Oberfeldwebel* (staff sergeant) who had called the snap parade met Buckwieg to announce that all were present and correct.

"And this one?" asked Buckwieg.

Few of the people who helped to form the work party in this escape could have guessed that George would use the idea in a much more sophisticated and courageous form a year or so later.

Two things of major significance had their beginnings in Stalag Luft I. Camp administration in the NCOs' compound had been a highly shaky affair. A group of senior, Regular NCOs had tried to run the show on the rather inadequate bases of Kings Regulations and Air Council Instructions. Without a doubt this system worked in its way, but it did not consolidate the various brands of airmen ranging from Regular NCOs to 'sprog' wartime-only sergeants.

It was at this moment that James Alexander Deans emerged at the head of what might be regarded as a spontaneous idea – the election of a town council to run the camp with German-speaking James Deans as its leader, or 'Man of Confidence' according to the German book.

This, coupled with the fact that Red Cross parcels were now coming in with greater regularity and that James Deans and his elected Camp Secretary with dozens of eager helpers were getting life organised, laid the first bricks of the firm base from which George Grimson and the emerging Escape Committee could work.

Another great event was the first illicit wireless news from home. This came through John Bristow's Mark I wonder, the radio receiver which brought the news from England and hope to many a temporarily-faint heart.

As already remarked, the radio was codenamed 'Canary' for security reasons and that was its name until the end of the war. The two last 'Canaries', one in a portable gramophone which still played records, the other in a mess tin, were brought home and now rest in the Royal Air Force Museum at Hendon.

All these radio sets bore the brand of genius, but none more so than the Mark I. Happy chance had brought John Bristow, the super mechanic-technician, into touch with David Young, BBC back-room boy. David produced a basic wiring circuit. John Bristow set out to scrounge the parts and to make others. Some limited working parties were still allowed, and when John Bristow volunteered as a dustman – "Temporary, acting/ unpaid" to quote him – he found a positive Ali Baba's Cave in the Barth dust-tip. One of the things he scrounged and got working was a small immersion heater, which suitably adapted could give him warm water for shaving or a quick brew-up.

But things like that were merely to keep himself occupied. His consuming interest was in the radio. If escape dominated the life of George

Grimson and others, the idea of a link with home filled John Bristow's waking and sleeping thoughts.

A tuning condenser was made from an old French mess-tin; the transformer was hand-wound from 'spare' wire taken from the German lighting system. It was a little large at first and had to be hidden in the false bottom of a jam tin used for rubbish, or 'gash' in RAF parlance. Smoothing condensers were made from the tin-foil tops of cigarette tins inserted between Bible leaves (the only source of thin India paper), then turned over at the ends and soldered. The whole was then boiled in paraffin wax from altar candles acquired in a most dubious way (some Communion wine was also 'seen off' at the same time).

But the great problem was to get valves. Everything else could be home-made, but not the 'Toobs' as 'Bris' insisted on calling them. A quick sleight of hand by Sandy Sands, another Regular, while he was working in the *Vorlager* left a German radio deficient of a full set of valves. There was no blitz search after this as we expected, probably because the loss was never reported for fear of punishment.

Another Bristow, Don, now an editorial executive in Fleet Street, took the first verbatim news to be received by us. It was not very cheerful, for the time of the war was bad and we British were on our own and knew it.

The great problem with the radio was smoothing condensers. "The rate of failure is about two in eight and we cannot guarantee a regular service until we get some shop-made ones," warned 'Bris'. That led to the first direct link between this great morale-builder – which George Grimson had quickly recognised it to be – and the Escape Committee. They had of necessity already established trading relations with certain Germans. In no time the components were forthcoming.

Perhaps the home-made earphones were one of the most interesting pieces of equipment. These lasted until the end of the war. The magnets were made by crushing razor blades and annealing them into a core, which was then wrapped in wire from an electric shaver. Diaphragms came from the ubiquitous thin seals on tinned cigarettes and the whole earphone was placed in a plastic tooth-powder container with a hole cut in the lid. The phones were then stuck in a scrum cap and you were in business.

Both the Escape Committee and Jimmy Deans were anxious to extract the maximum effect from the radio as a morale-builder. So, while the Mark II set was being built, a corps of readers was formed and trained to deliver the news in the unemotional tones of the BBC. Their instructor was Peter J. M. Thomas, then a Sergeant Pilot, now MP and sometime Minister for Wales. When finished and installed, the Mark II was operated every night from then on, except when we were travelling from prison to prison.

With the news going out on a regular and controlled basis, there was a steady rise in morale and a greater willingness to co-operate with a now exceedingly active Escape Committee. Map makers appeared and plied their trade. Forgers, one of whom was in time of peace a distinguished heraldic painter, were organised into working parties. The less skilful were employed in tapping needles with a hammer to get the molecules all pointing one way, thereby creating magnetic needles. The master craftsmen, many of whom were ex-boy apprentices of the Service – 'the Trenchard Brats' – dug out their basic skills and made beautifully constructed marching compasses from bakelite toothpaste containers.

Things were really beginning to tick.

Chapter 4

A BETTER Christmas was promised in 1941, for Red Cross parcels were arriving regularly. The contents of these were vital, not only as food, but for the many other ways in which they could be utilised. Steve Bevan from the RNZAF, for instance, used the tins to make a thermally insulated oven which fitted on top of a stove to warm the hut. John Bristow cooked the tins down to get the solder out of them for his radios and his other great spare-time project, a flint and steel ignition petrol engine.

For the Escape Committee, the Red Cross parcels were a godsend in a number of ways. Unpierced tins were hidden away for escape food, chocolate from personal parcels from home was stored for the same reason. But these supplies had another very important use – for trading with the Germans who, in the land of *ersatz*, longed for certain 'goodies' to take home on leave to their families. Jimmy Deans, Grimson and other members of the Escape Committee already recognised this as a weapon for use against an enemy forbidden to trade with prisoners, especially later when a German caught trading usually got a posting to the dreaded Eastern Front. The sophisticated development of bribery and corruption of the enemy was to come much later. Still, this was the start.

On 21st December 1941, George wrote to his brother John: "By the time you get this, Christmas will be over, but have a belated one on me." Earlier he had asked his brother for a number of things, including clothing for his personal parcel. Clothing was of the greatest importance to the escaper, especially anything that could be re-tailored in the camp to give it a civilian look.

"Don't worry unduly," said George about this list, "but if you can get them for me I shall be set up in clothes for a long time and you would not have to worry for a couple of years."

Whatever some of the pundits might have said at the time, it was clear that George was planning a long way ahead. He believed it was going to be a long war and frequently said as much. Also he was busy learning German and he knew the job would take him time, particularly as he was involved in so many other activities connected with escape. The end of this letter-card is typical of the independent George. He wanted favours from no one, not even his greatly beloved brother. "You will get the money OK," he adds. "Don't be annoyed about it, but I can't let you keep paying out for me."

Another regular NCO, the amiable, unruffled but very much on-the-ball Alfie Fripp, was playing an important role in the Red Cross store. He supervised the distribution of parcels to the British NCOs while the German staff kept an eye on him. Alfie could, and still can, charm the birds out of the trees, so it was not surprising that a proportion of un-pierced tins made their way into the hands of the Escape Committee, even though the Germans had strict orders to prevent this because they knew whole tins could be used for escape.

Opened tins were also helpful. They could be used for almost everything from digging to making air ducts for tunnels. Through a line of connected milk tins, for instance, air could be pumped to the tunnel face.

Christmas, 1941, was memorable in another way. The Senior British Officer from the adjoining officers' compound, 'Wings' Day, was allowed to come over and talk to us. Publicly he said: "The war has *not* finished for you. You are still members of the Royal Air Force. Tough times are ahead, and you can win through. But always remember this: loyalty, toleration and co-operation are the key words in your existence." But in the few private words he was able to have, Wings took a much more aggressive line. "Escape," he urged us. "Keep on trying. Keep the buggers busy if that's the only thing you can do. I know it is tougher for you as NCOs, but don't give in an inch."

As the year went on its way, John Bristow's radio sets were modified and, under James ('King Dixie') Deans, camp organisation steadily improved. Concerts were started, tunnels dug and various escape schemes were hatched out. George kept mainly in the background – planning, scheming and perfecting his knowledge of German ready for *The Day*. That his job was helped by the lift in morale 'Dixie' Deans had generated by putting the camp on a level administrative keel, George was quick to recognise.

Several incidents of note marked the blazing summer of 1941. Escapers in the spring and men out on working parties garnering intelligence had come back with the news that an escape to the east was out of the question. They had walked into areas full of strong formations of German troops. Tales were told of petrol supply tanks jacked up by the roadside and of tanks and SP guns tucked neatly away in just the sort of cover that an escaping prisoner must use.

Early in the year George had written to his mother saying that he had received her letter posted before Christmas. He mentioned trouble with his address, but did not say that it had been due to his attempted escape, banishment to Lamsdorf and subsequent return to Barth. He had not received any parcels from her, probably for the same reason. Of these, he wrote: "I must have those clothes I asked for. Send them if you can, but I know it is very difficult, so don't worry unduly." Good clothes were so essential. One of the many things that could give an escaper away was a scruffy appearance. It is obvious why they were uppermost in George's mind. Referring guardedly to some of his already exciting experiences, he told his mother: "I'll have some yarns to tell you when I see you and they'll have you laughing for a month. Do you know I don't think I'd have missed this place for a fortune. You would have laughed to death seeing me do fourteen days solitary just for taking an unauthorised stroll through the woods." Thus George light-heartedly passed off an abortive attempt to get back.

The war in the outside world still impinged on us. One big event in 1941 was the sinking of the old *Hood* by the modern *Bismarck*. The Germans had installed radios around the camp over which they made *Sondermeldungen* – special announcements – of big events. So high was morale by this time, however, that the ancient out-gunned British ship was barely on the bottom before the Kriegies were laying bets with the Germans that Churchill would destroy the German before she could get back to safety. Janner Purchase, a one-time Shotley boy of the Fleet Air Arm, was even going round offering five to one on her destruction. To give them their due the Germans were sometimes good losers and actually broadcast over the camp loud-speaker system the last messages alleged to have been transmitted by the *Bismarck* when she was overwhelmed by the avenging Royal Navy. Although the NCOs' camp admired the bravery of the German ship's crew, Kriegie humour with its strange brand of assumed cruelty came uppermost and more than one NCO got seven days' solitary on bread and water for asking the Jerries whether they wanted to buy a battleship.

Another great moment which set the loud-speakers blaring was the invasion of Russia on 22nd June 1941. It was high summer on the Baltic and those who were not digging tunnels were lazing in the sun or doing a bit of 'goon baiting'. "You've had it now", shouted Ron West to the sentry on the watch tower. The goon shouted back in good-humoured German and George translated. "He says they'll be at the gates of Moscow in five weeks – and he may be bloody right, so let's keep things going. We mustn't relax, not for any reason." The goon was right. They were at the gates of Moscow in a few weeks. Only luck, the weather and failure in German logistics saved the Russians from the occupation of Moscow.

That winter found the Germans strangely unprepared. The NCO prisoners who still had Irving fur-lined leather jackets were ordered to hand them over, and they were duly collected; but every one of them was slashed to pieces with razor blades. When the Germans unpacked their loot ready to send to their freezing comrades on the East Front, their howls of rage could be heard all over the compound. As a result, minor irritations were imposed, like cutting the lights off at certain hours of the afternoon and evening and then suddenly putting them on at night. Another trick was to cut off water supplies, which resulted in a complete freeze-up. One bucket of hot water was issued per barrack room every day and cards were drawn for turns to wash in it. Rupert Greenhalgh, survivor of one of those ghastly two-seat Defiant aircraft, described his share at number 24 as "rather like washing in liquid Black Magic".

We were soon lousy, too, and although the Germans made some attempts to de-louse us by removing all our hair, giving us brief showers and cooking our clothing, all they really did was to hatch out the lice eggs in the seams. They were soon busy biting again. All of which suited George. "Let 'em have it hard," he was heard to observe, "the harder it gets the more they'll hate the Jerry and the more they'll try and escape. Suits me." We soon found, however, that the best de-louser was the extreme cold; if you hung your clothes outside at night in Baltic minus temperature not even a louse could stay alive.

Peter Fox, another keen escaper, added to this recipe by jumping out of the window every morning when the shutters were taken down and rolling naked in the snow, scrubbing himself with it. "It's lovely," he shouted, "it's wonderful. You want to try it." A few did at first, but the number soon dwindled to just Peter. Anyway he was one of the few fighter types in the camp, whereas the rest of us were bomber types! And every good bomber type knows that you have to be a little bit cracked to be a fighter type.

Christmas, 1941, was a great one, I remember. The weather was reasonable, we were receiving Red Cross parcels, the Germans were bogged down in Russia and not feeling so confident. Men were waiting for the spring, when the escape fever really stirred in the blood, although we were beginning to realise that early autumn was the best time, as the 'walkers' could live on crops from the fields.

We had also by now received a padre, a French-Canadian Roman Catholic priest, who had been taken aboard the U-boat which sank the liner *Egypt* and brought back to Germany. He was a man of great moral courage who stood up to the Germans from the very beginning. In fact, they eventually shifted him to a civilian internees' camp, as the *Abwehr* were suspicious of his activities. The comfort and cheer that he gave to everyone whatever their denomination is remembered with warmth by many of us to this day. His absolute serenity and cheerfulness were a tonic. When we were all lousy, he saved at least one man's sanity. "Do you know," he observed quietly, "that St Francis of Assisi used to call lice 'the pearls of poverty'?" Somehow it made you feel less lousy.

As the padre was the only one in the camp with a room to himself, it was from here that the radio was operated. While the operator got in touch with England and took down the news, the padre quietly sat and prayed. Before the set was back in its hiding place, there was always a cup of tea or cocoa on hand and Padre Goudereau never once asked what the news was; this was kept secret until the following midday for security reasons. The padre had in fact been trained as a missionary and had been on his way to minister to the Bantu. He was once heard to remark drily to one of his flock that his task was to minister to the pagan and the unknowing, so perhaps God in His wisdom had re-routed him.

In spite of lice, crowded conditions and a low diet the prisoners of war kept remarkably fit. There was little sickness and no epidemics, which was just as well as the Germans had not seen fit to bless us with a medical officer at that time. We had to rely instead on the local doctor, who proudly displayed his Party badge and made it pretty clear that he did not think much of us. The feeling was mutual.

But an epidemic of typhus was sweeping through Eastern Europe and the Germans were rightly scared. Only one case was recorded among the NCO prisoners, that of Ferdie Farrans. Ferdie was one of the many camp eccentrics and it was recognised that he had every right to be so. First he was a pilot of that God-awful monstrosity of the air, known as the Hampden; secondly he had been shot down twice – once by Spitfire pilots over the Firth of Forth who mistook the Hampden for a Messerschmitt 110, and again by the Germans. Now he had typhus and was duly wheeled off to isolation hospital, which in Germany was grim for the Germans, let alone for us.

Anyway, Ferdie's illness so put the breeze up the camp staff that for days they brought the prisoners' rations on a cart to the gate of the *Lager*, opened the gate and retired hurriedly to a watchful distance, while the prisoners brought the cart into the camp and unloaded the rations. The Germans then fetched the empty cart to the jeers of the prisoners. "No guts, windy," we chorused.

There was no little apprehension inside the wire too. A sergeant who had escaped from medical college to join up – and now a 'great' in Harley Street – comforted many by explaining it was quite possible to 'think' oneself into the early-stage symptoms of the disease without really having it. Things quietened down after that.

Generally it was not a good winter for escape, especially with typhus raging outside. But spring was in the air and hopes abounding. Perhaps what triggered them off was the return to the camp of a cured Ferdie Farrans. As he remarked, if Spitfires and Messerschmitts couldn't knock him off, no bloody little German bug was going to do it!

The organisation of general camp life had now been firmly consolidated by James Deans. He had an office staff and sub-committees running everything from entertainment to education. His own closely-guarded secret link with Grimson and the Escape Committee, and of course a well-organised BBC news service, were weapons he controlled. The news service went on in spite of the fact that John Bristow suddenly developed appendicitis and was carted off from the camp on a stretcher for treatment in a German hospital. To our amazement he returned only two days later, walking doubled up and carrying his own kit. We rushed to help him. He was the same irrepressible Bristow.

"There's one thing to be said for the squareheads," he remarked, "straight in, whip your appendix out, 24 hours in bed and there you are on your feet as good as new." His friends took his kit.

"You don't half notice things on the ground when you have to walk in this position," he remarked as he made his way to his hut. "I'll get into my pit and see if I can straighten out. It's been quite a walk."

Indeed it had. A German truck had dumped him at the outer gates of the *Vorlager* with his kit and, once he had been signed for, he had had to walk into the NCOs' compound. No German helped him carry his kit or his straw mattress.

Chapter 5

WITH the spring of 1942 came news of the building of a new camp at Sagan to which we were to move. The Germans told us with glee that it was especially for Air Force prisoners and was "completely escape-proof". George Grimson, 'Aussie' Lascelles, 'Wimpy' Wootton and other members of the Escape Committee grinned and waited. They had already heard the news because by now the camp organisation had built up an intelligence system which stretched beyond the confines of the wire.

A great deal of information concerning the passes and ration cards required by anyone who proposed to travel in the 'Third and Last' came from guards, who either did not approve of the Nazi party or who could be persuaded by the 'traders' to part with knowledge for cigarettes and chocolate, now arriving in increasing quantities through the Red Cross service. A large volume of local knowledge was gathered by 'Aussie' Lascelles. For some reason he had won the German trust and was allowed to take out a small working party which invariably included 'Wimpy' Wootton and certain other dedicated escapers. At this stage their aim was not to escape but to collect intelligence, which they did with outstanding success. Some of their information about work going on at the nearby rocket experimental station was to be of vital importance to Bomber Command Intelligence at home. Subsequently we were sorry we were not still at Barth when Peenemünde suffered its devastating clobbering by Bomber Command, which knocked off a number of German scientists, although the top man, von Braun, survived – which was probably just as well for the success of the United States space programme of later years.

'Aussie's' squad still worked in the fish-canning factory, and it was from here that he made his subsequent escape. Unfortunately, it proved unsuccessful. To make matters worse he fell into the hands of the Gestapo, who promptly accused him of being a spy. 'Aussie' contrived to stay behind when the party moved off back to camp, though how the Jerries failed to miss him or how he managed to conceal his vast bulk even in the confines of the factory was a mystery to us all. During the night he emerged from the tinned fish and promptly set course for an aerodrome which intelligence had located some miles from the camp.

A former Hudson pilot with pre-war experience of flying out in the Australian bush, 'Aussie' was confident that if he could 'borrow' one of the light aircraft used there for training pilots *ab initio* and start it, he would have no difficulty in flying to Sweden. He reached the aerodrome, located his plane and seemed set for freedom. It was bad luck that an unusually alert guard, having a quiet smoke inside a hangar, spotted him and he was soon undergoing a really tough interrogation.

It was as well that camp intelligence heard at once of his predicament. Pressure was put on the Germans by George Grimson through 'Dixie' Deans and a message got through to the Protecting Power. Official questions were asked. The result was that a thinner, less ebullient 'Aussie' was duly returned to the camp. He would never say much about what had happened to him, even to close friends like Flockhart and Grimson. He had been given a rough time.

At any rate, the honeymoon between 'Aussie' and the Jerries was now over and the fish factory parties came to a sudden end. 'Aussie' resumed his anti-German campaign, which even for a Kriegie was extreme. He just hated Jerries and believed in hitting them anywhere and everywhere and as often as possible.

With his short neck, large egg-shaped head and body of a well-bred shorthorn bull, 'Aussie' looked and was formidable. On summer nights he would keep a self-imposed vigil at the hut window after curfew until he saw one of the security guards, known as ferrets, go to work. Under each hut a narrow tunnel had been dug and the ferret's job was to go down the tunnel and ensure that no illicit digging operations were in progress under the hut floor. At night it must have been eerie work. As soon as the ferret had gone to ground, 'Aussie' would nip out of the window and position a nicely-tangled piece of barbed wire in the tunnel. Then he would let fly an aboriginal shriek down the hole. The ferret would stampede up the tunnel in terror and emerge looking as if he had been having a fight with a tiger.

'Aussie' Lascelles pursued the persecution of ferrets with a relentless Antipodean humour. Later, at Heydekrug, he managed to obtain a quantity of acetylene powder from an unsuspecting German on the grounds that he needed it for lighting. Nothing was further from 'Aussie's' thoughts, however. He needed it for his favourite sport. Soon enthusiastic helpers in the escapers' hut had a hole bored in the floor and the acetylene powder spread thickly in the inspection trench beneath the hut. That night, as soon as the ferret was known to be underneath the hut, 'Aussie' put liquid – most definitely not water – on the acetylene. A choking ferret dashed from beneath the hut. Next day the German Commandant solemnly complained to Jimmy Deans that we had broken the Geneva Convention by the use of gas warfare! And he wasn't joking either, which made it funnier still.

Complaisance or boredom or both were the greatest enemies to overcome at this time and Grimson and the rest of the Escape Committee were anxious to move on to the new camp before everyone settled down too much. Nevertheless, although the prisoners appeared to be taking it easy, most of them were engaged actively in 'goon-baiting' in the 'Aussie' Lascelles style and the guards had a pretty thin time. Perhaps too, the ancillary activities like education and the theatre might have seemed a little frivolous to an utterly devoted escaper like George when he was completely immersed in planning the fight against the common enemy.

George Grimson welcomed the idea of a move for another reason. To him an 'escape-proof' camp was a direct challenge, particularly as he knew by this time that it was in Silesia, and the Sudeten mountains were not far away.

We moved on what was known to us as 'Arry 'Itler's' birthday, 20th April 1942. The train journey to Silesia was protracted and uncomfortable. We were herded into cattle-trucks, most of them stolen French rolling stock. Each truck was divided into three by barbed wire. Forty prisoners were packed in each of the end compartments, while five or six heavily-armed German guards rested with a bit more comfort in the middle section. The radio travelled in a concertina, which still played although missing some notes in the bass register. Other secret equipment was carefully hidden – for example, in the false bottoms of tins. Nothing of any importance was detected by the German security staff at 'escape-proof' Sagan when we arrived.

Train journeys were always good vehicles for escape and it was inevitable that a number of attempts were made, all unsuccessful unfortunately. One effort seized on the fact that a lot of German railway trucks needed re-flooring, where holes had been broken in the floor boards. The ever-enterprising Harry Leggatt had had himself nailed up in one of the many boxes carrying camp material and managed to get out this way en route, but was soon recaptured and duly rejoined us after we arrived.

During the move we also managed to acquire all the documents and personal property of *Gefreiter* Günther Wagner, a smart-alec guard who was to receive official treatment later on. Among his papers was a fascinating and no doubt somewhat fictitious family tree going back some generations. This was designed to prove that he had no taint of Jewish blood. Apparently a document of this type was a must for any good Nazi. We kept a close eye on Wagner after that.

The escorting guards were only too relieved to get us handed over in the reception area at Sagan. On our side spirits were high. Even the deplorably uncomfortable journey had failed to depress us. George's dry reaction came sometime during the middle of the journey, when a disgruntled voice said: "Forty hommes, eight chevaux it says outside." "Shut up or they'll hear you and shove bleeding horses in as well," replied George.

At Sagan we were placed in a compound adjoining the officers' pen. As we soon had the radio working, Chief Petty Officer Alex, or 'Buggy' Brims, another former Shotley Boy steeped in the Navy way of doing things, had the job of 'zogging' (a form of short semaphore) the news to the officers' compound every day. This in itself was a lift-up for the sergeants. We were the radio wizards and what is more we felt that we were doing something to repay the officers for the fund they had raised and for all they had done to help us.

Gradually things got going and more and more Air Force prisoners joined the camp from other prisons where they had been held. One of the most remarkable of these was Alan Morris, who spoke perfect German. He and George had met at Lamsdorf and they immediately formed a team. It was clear that the next break would be a Morris-Grimson effort – and here the Germans really had dropped a clanger. All their efforts to reduce German manpower wasted in looking after the Air Force prisoners had succeeded only in collecting under one roof the worst or best, depending from which side you viewed the situation. It was to be the source of much trouble to the natives in the months ahead.

In the officers' compound the firm of 'Wings' Day, Roger Bushell and James Buckley was happily united in doing the Germans a mischief. This culminated in the successful Wooden Horse escape, from which all three officers got home, and in the great Sagan tunnel where another three made it against the fifty-one killed by the Gestapo. In the NCOs' compound even more trouble was building up, for George and the other members who made up the nucleus of the Escape Committee were encountering fresh kindred souls.

Grimson and Morris and others of their team had to keep in the background, out of the way of the Germans. It was on Jock Alexander, one of the IIIe escapologists, and on the organisation he formed to back up the Escape Committee that much too much limelight had unfortunately to fall, because it made him well-known to the Germans. He deserves a special place in any book about George Grimson, for without his organising ability and dedication the subsequent Heydekrug 'underground railway' or escape route would have had a much more difficult time. Shot down over Bremen in August 1941, Jock had immediately gone on the run. Back at home in England at this time they were not really sufficiently briefed to teach escape and evasion, so Jock had none of the aids like a concentrated food-pack and other accessories which became commonplace equipment later.

His first stop after bailing out was a barn where he acquired a black cloth overcoat to cover his uniform. A cap from a scarecrow encountered in a nearby field helped a bit more. As soon as he hit ground, Jock knew what he wanted to do – make his way to Lübeck and get aboard a ship for Sweden.

At first it seemed that luck was on his side, especially when he 'found' an unused bicycle outside a pub. He then set off to cycle the 120 miles to Lübeck. Short of food, he found that he had to exist on apples, for the Germans line many of their roads with apple trees. As he was to observe ruefully later: "An apple a day might keep the doctor away, but an apple diet is insufferable. In the end I just couldn't eat any more – my stomach rejected them." Frequently, too, he had to slake his thirst from a puddle.

Pushing on with determination through the outskirts of Hamburg he managed to steal some bread from a baker's van. This was the only real food he had had in two days. Finally at Lübeck he managed to get to the harbour and board a ship. In one cabin the ravenous escaper helped himself to bread and jam. In another he found a sponge cake.

But something about the ship – probably the arrival of a drunken German sailor – started Jock's alarm bells ringing. While the sailor was being ill, he slipped off the ship and hid ashore. Next morning he watched the ship sail. She was wearing the Nazi Swastika flag.

His next choice was a three-masted Swedish schooner. Jock was soon aboard and tucked away under the inboard end of the bowsprit. Well out to sea the ship was stopped and searched by the Germans and Jock was found. A week or so later he was at the Wehrmacht camp of IIIe at Kirchhain, where through a tunnel he was to make his second effort to escape along with fifty others.

At about the same time, a number of other types who had somehow got mis-routed to an Army camp, Stalag IXc, arrived at Sagan. They had proved too much for the camp guards and one or two of the inmates, who had other ideas about 'goon-baiting' and regular escapes. Among them was the indestructible, belligerent Tony Hunter of cooler fame, whose Spitfire had been hacked down over France – "by a sprog who was shooting at the wing leader and made a wrong deflection", complained Tony.

During the first few weeks, conditions at Sagan were a little chaotic. Had we been as organised for escape as we were later, the Germans would soon have discovered that the place was full of bolt holes. Typical was the empty latrine from which the late Bill Williams, Ron West and Gerry Tipping began to burrow their way. The only trouble was that the camp was receiving so many prisoners, especially after the 1,000 bomber raid on Cologne, that the latrine was in use before the 'moler', or quickly-built shallow tunnel, could get through the wire. In the rueful summation of Gerry Tipping: "Our efforts in the *Abort* were aborted."

One of the things which worried Jock Alexander most was illicit trading with the enemy, particularly now that the Red Cross routes had been re-organised and parcels were coming through. This had boiled up again following the move. Paddy Flockhart had industriously cultivated a German named Schmidt who was also called 'Mudgutz' by the Kriegies because of his podgy appearance. But he had been useful in bringing in radio parts for John Bristow. Other prisoners started to establish their contacts, too. In the end it was clear to everyone, and especially to men like George Grimson, that uncontrolled trading would only result in competition and dissipation of effort in the cause of escape.

In the officers' compound it had been relatively easy to exercise this type of discipline. 'Dixie' Deans, Alexander and Grimson now evolved a scheme which, by drawing everyone into the orbit of the escape attempts, would without endangering their secrecy enable trading to be channelled through one route controlled by the Escape Committee. Thus the Tally-Ho Club was born.

Not only was the need and duty of all prisoners to help escape impressed upon everyone; a lot of useful jobs were handed out to be done when the order was given. The whole thing was approached in the particularly light-hearted way in which the old RAF used to disguise its more deadly intentions.

If any prisoner saw a German enter a barrack block, it was his duty to shout "goons-up" or later Tally-Ho, the famous fighter hunting cry that had swept the Germans out of the English skies. This was good fun. John Bristow would promptly put away his soldering iron and concentrate on something more or less innocent, like the famous hand-made clock he produced. Forgers, map makers and other helpers would turn to more blameless business. Tailors would switch to a job for the next play in the theatre and even enlist the help of the odd German in getting sewing material for them.

All this was useful and a large step towards perfecting the hundred per cent escape machine required by George and his associates. Later a 'duty pilot' system was introduced. As soon as a German goon or ferret entered the camp, he was immediately tailed by one of the 'duty flight' who reported to 'flight control' at regular intervals through a system of runners. So effective was this system, that it became the custom for the head of the *Abwehr* himself, Hermann Glemnitz, to report to the 'flight controller' whenever he entered the camp and wanted to know the whereabouts of any of his men!

There were three very fine men on the German side at Sagan and I should record that none of my comment on the natives in general apply to them. *Feldwebel* Glemnitz, a jovial giant of a man, managed in an extra-ordinary way to combine exemplary duty to his own Service with treatment of his prisoners as though they were his own men. His behaviour was impeccable and his good humour infectious. Another such was the Commandant, *Oberst* von Lindeiner-Wildau. He too behaved towards us with scrupulous correctness and admitted it was the duty of every man to attempt escape. That swine Himmler tried to get him murdered after the big Sagan escape. The last of the trio was *Hauptmann* Pieber, an Austrian. Once a dedicated Nazi, he had like many of the more intelligent Germans become thoroughly disillusioned with the Monster with the Moustache and his brood of junior Monsters like Fatty Göring. All in all, Sagan was a remarkable camp, for it contained men who were the best of their respective warring races.

Chapter 6

THE arrival of the party from Camp IIIe at Kirchhain was especially fortuitous for the escapers and by the same token quite disastrous for the enemy. Kirchhain had housed not only Jock Alexander, but also a group of NCOs who had been the first to make a mass escape by tunnel.

In claiming the first break-out for the NCOs, I do not disparage in any way the much bigger tunnel break by our officers at Sagan later in March 1944, which resulted in three men getting home. All the same, the story of the escape at Kirchhain is worth telling if only because of its influence in persuading George to establish an escape route and the fund of new experience it added.

There were, of course, other escape routes in Europe, but none on the eastern side where we were. In occupied Holland, Belgium and France, the routes were organised and nurtured from Headquarters back in Britain. But most of the people who used these routes were evaders, not escapers.

There is a fine distinction between these two classes of men of courage. An evader was a man who was lucky enough to get away by making touch with an escape route before he could be caught and thrown into a prison camp. The escaper was a man who had failed to avoid the 'bag', usually because he was shot down many miles inside Germany. When he got out of the bag he was an escaper. On the run he became an evader.

The Grimson underground escape route was perforce to be a do-it-yourself job, planned from inside prison camp. A grim fact should here be noticed about the escape routes of Europe. More than 23,000 Allied service men passed along them: and for everyone of these men who got home, on average four-and-a-half French, Belgian or Dutch men, women and children were sent to the hells of Belsen, Dachau or similar 'corrective establishments'. Not very many of these brave and devoted people returned to their homes. But back to Kirchhain. . . .

The camp was situated near Finsterwalde, at a spot where two main railway lines, from Halle to Cottbus and Dresden to Berlin, intersect. It was built on the usual lines, four single-storey huts (brick-built in this case), surrounded by a warning wire and an outer double wire fence. This was another 'Green-Job' camp. As jailers, the Wehrmacht were worse than the Luftwaffe, who did have some gentlemen among them.

In July 1941, the first batch of RAF NCOs was transferred to Kirchhain.

They were joined later by others, until by August the prisoner ration strength stood at about 200 hungry airmen.

The first escape attempt came within three months, when a number of Kriegies discovered that a hole made through the wall of one of the barracks would open on to the rifle range. This was outside the main German compound and not surrounded by wire. Operations were started at once and the working parties got down to 'mouseholing' the wall with an iron spike, the rest of us covering the noise by community singing in the open which the Germans were invited to attend. They did so and the *Abwehr* happily sat listening to spirited renderings of old British songs which ended only when the signal was received that the hole was completed. This was an early example of all-round co-operation and the practice of diversions.

Between ten and eleven o'clock that night the loose bricks which had been replaced were pushed out and the hole opened up. Twelve men went out.

They were ill-prepared. Maps were few, compasses and other escape aids were even fewer and food was extremely short. All the escapers had was a small quantity of German black bread which had been saved from their meagre daily ration, since no Red Cross parcels had yet arrived. None had any documents. Yet here they were outside and loose in the middle of Germany. It was a brave effort but doomed to failure.

The Germans discovered the break in the early hours of the following morning, when one of the escapers was found walking quite blatantly through the middle of a nearby village. He was actually whistling an English tune. Within five days all the others had been caught and were back in the cooler.

Meantime the local natives had had a full night of alarms and excursions. 'Cigars' had been handed out all round. They had lost a lot of sleep – and their tempers too, as the Kriegies were to discover next morning.

Instead of the normal roll call, the prisoners found themselves confronted by a horde of German troops, who were paraded in front of them. Ostentatiously the German soldiers were ordered to 'put one up the spout' of their rifles. They looked ready for murder.

The British were now forced to discard their footwear and don *Stiefeln*, wooden shoes and boots which the natives use in villages in the winter and of which a supply had been brought into the compound. In these the prisoners were ordered to double-march inside a ring of armed guards by an officer with a drawn pistol. Faster and faster he ordered the prisoners to go. Men who kicked off the uncomfortable wooden clogs to run in bare feet were made to put them back on. Prisoners who fainted from pain, or from fatigue due to the low rations, had to be supported by their comrades. While all this was going on, the barracks were being searched to the accompaniment of some senseless destruction, like tearing books apart and smashing pictures. The following morning two prisoners who were late on parade were punished with an hour of the 'clog dance'. This, decided the camp in general and Jock Alexander and other escapers in particular, was not to be endured.

A site for a new attempt was immediately chosen. Two men in the camp, it turned out, had mining experience and they were told off to master-mind the building of a tunnel. This little operation was to give the Germans the reddest neck they had had "since Napoleon knocked the stuffing out of them way back", as one prisoner put it.

A shaft about four feet square was sunk vertically to a depth of six feet at a point under the east wall of No 2 barrack. After the shaft had been built, the tunnel proper was begun from just below the foundations of the barrack wall. Shoring was done with bed-boards.

The Germans had thoughtfully provided all prisoners with double- or treble-tiered wooden beds. The actual base of the bed, upon which the straw-filled palliasses rested, was made up of single boards, each about six inches wide by three feet long. These bed-boards were ideal supports for tunnel roofs and walls. The digging teams worked by the light of fat lamps, home-made from old tins filled with oil or margarine with pieces of cloth or pyjama cord for wicks. Contributions of equipment came from all over the camp, not just from the tunnellers.

The work progressed, but before long breathing became a problem and the diggers found it hard to stay alive; shortage of oxygen meant, too, that the lamps would not stay alight. Airholes, small but risky, had to be dug through the roof of the tunnel and at the end of each day's working they were covered with an apparently casually-placed stone or brick. Many of the team selected to keep watch on German activities and generally safe-guard the tunnellers had heart-stopping moments when a German guard strolled past the airholes from time to time. But this was a Green-Job camp and the staff were not so much on their toes as they were in the special Luftwaffe camps. One useful purpose served by the ventilation holes was to keep the tunnel straight – always a problem in this kind of operation.

Already, the escapers had realised the importance of intelligence, particularly as it affected the prisoners inside. In due course several tame goons were found. When one of these gave warning that an intensive search was pending, it was decided to stop all digging and hide the tunnel entrance with boards covered by several feet of sand and soil. The search duly took place and was far more efficient and thorough than the normal ones. Escape hoards of chocolate, dried food and other rations were discovered and duly confiscated. But the tunnel remained undiscovered. While the thoroughly satisfied Jerries departed on their way rejoicing –

and doubtless calculating their share of the stolen rations – the prisoners got ready to start again.

Time was not on their side, however. At the beginning of May, intelligence learned that the enemy was about to evacuate the camp, probably within the week.

Here was a problem for the escapers. At this time the tunnel was only half-way to freedom. Chances were ruefully measured, but they could only come up with one answer – dig. Dig: and get everyone in the camp to help passing back the soil and getting rid of it.

The next blow fell on 8th May, when 100 prisoners were transferred from Kirchhain to the NCOs' compound at Sagan. Unfortunately, they included some of the escapers and several of the engineers. The efforts made by the diggers had been so prodigious that by now the tunnel reached to within 60 feet of the perimeter wire.

With the knowledge that the final evacuation of the camp was sheduled to take place in four or five days' time, new diggers were recruited and again all prisoners in the camp took some part in the last frenzied 'blitz' on the tunnelling work. By 11th May, the perimeter had been reached; but even now there were more problems because of patrolling sentries who interrupted the work as they walked up and down the wire. Too much was at stake now to get caught out by the sharp ears of a bright sentry, and it was just possible that there might be some eager beaver in the ranks of the Green Jobs who was grooming himself for stardom.

Meantime, inside the camp preparations for escape were made. By vote it was decided that the principal diggers should go first, followed by the more prominent members of the support team. The rest of the places were decided by ballot.

When darkness came on the night of 11th May, the get-away hole was broken just outside the fence and the first two men crawled away into the darkness beyond the area lit by the boundary lights. This process continued through the night and by dawn 52 men had left the tunnel.

Amazingly enough, the Germans were late in discovering the first mass escape of the war. Early on the morning of 12th May, as the last pair out were rapidly making their way to cover, the Germans entered the camp and asked for the British Camp Leader. They wanted, they said, to arrange the move to Sagan with his help – which was a bit difficult as the Camp Leader was now well on his way in the open.

To give the escapers more time, the prisoners refused to get up. This, of course, sparked off the usual display of Jerry excitement, which turned to consternation when the Germans eventually forced their captives out of bed to parade for counting. The normal number of prisoners had plainly dwindled somewhat. Now a real outburst of Jerry panic set in – shouting, yelling and mounting hysteria punctuated by shrilling whistles.

It was not until much later, while the Germans were still busily searching in the camp, that the exit hole was discovered by a guard patrolling outside the wire. Even then the Germans were baffled and could not discover the entrance to the tunnel inside the camp. Eventually one poor trembling ferret was persuaded down the outside hole and made his way along the 230 feet of tunnel to the entrance inside the camp.

This, the first of the big tunnels, was a masterpiece in its own rather unsophisticated way. There was no electric light and no air pump such as the officers were later to use at Sagan. But the tunnel was very long as tunnels went, shored with timber and dug by hand. Prison camp security men came down from Berlin to inspect and photograph this remarkable tribute to Kriegie engineering. It was obvious that they were impressed, but not so impressed as the Commandant, officers and security men of the camp who were given their 'cigars to smoke' by a very brusque Senior Gentleman from the Prisoner of War Command of the German Army.

It would have been happy to relate that after all this effort at least one escaper had got home, but such was not the case. All were recaptured. Nevertheless the prisoners had achieved something tantamount to a victory: the very magnitude of the escape had set all Germany humming. Over hundreds of square miles, troops, police, home guard and even the Hitler Jugend were employed for days searching for escapers. This diversion of German manpower, machines and organisation was, for obvious reasons, a primary aim of all escape attempts.

Some of the prisoners were recaptured in a few hours, but it took another ten days to round up the lot. There was one casualty. Two Canadians who had travelled together were alseep in a wood by a railway siding near Dresden when they were awakened by a German policeman. They stood up with their hands above their heads, then one of them, Sergeant H. Calpert, who spoke a few words of German, asked permission to put on his boots. He dropped one hand to point at his feet, whereat the German shot him dead.

All the other escapers were returned to the camp and later in the month transferred to the NCOs' camp at Sagan. A worthier band of recruits for escape could hardly have been found. They had much to avenge, not only the death of a comrade, but also the *Stiefeln* drill, as well as other indignities.

There were lessons to be drawn from every escape attempt, whether successful or not, presented by the thoughtful, and Jock Alexander was certainly one of them. He, Grimson, Morris and the rest of the new and enlarged Escape Committee now assembled in Sagan pondered the various difficulties. Even more important than getting out, though obviously basic, was staying out. It was also plainly important to get someone home. Any prisoner who made it back to Britain would be loaded with intelligence picked up on his travels. He might not even be aware of some of it, though with his co-operation it could be pieced together by skilful interrogators. It was also becoming clear, and would soon become even more evident, that the 'free traveller' in Hitler's Europe would need not only a knowledge of the language but passports, identification papers, ration cards and all the other paraphernalia of a country at war. That he would also need maps, compasses, concentrated food and other aids was obvious in any case.

With new experience and our numbers increasing by transfers from other camps, apart from a regular new intake as bomber raids intensified, we were ripe to cause trouble. It was not long in coming to the Germans.

Grimson, now solidly teamed with Alan Morris and Jock Alexander, was steadily perfecting his German. To this end he took on various jobs about the camp and the Germans were almost beginning to regard him naively as a reformed character. At last things were also happening in England. Maps, compasses and other escape equipment were now finding their way through to us. These consignments arrived hidden carefully by methods which I do not propose to mention as they might help a future enemy. But it was still the job of the genial Alfie Fripp, working in the Red Cross hut in the *Vorlager*, to get them out of the examination room and into the hands of the Escape Committee. This was done by a mixture of bribery and charm at which that ex-Halton apprentice was a pastmaster, with his German captors.

Here, as elsewhere, the now controlled illicit trading proceeded alongside dealings of a quite different character. There was now a small number of Germans who were becoming positively anti-Hitler and were prepared to help us. They were brave men who risked torture and death in their efforts to assist the escapers and they should not be forgotten. Nor should the key man of the trading organisation be overlooked. Sergeant Nat Leaman, a Londoner from the 'rag trade' and a member of the Jewish faith and proud of it, ran the trading group with great distinction, knowing that if he were caught a special fate might await him because of his religion. His natural trading instinct and his knowledge of several languages including perfect German were his stock in trade. His greatest asset, however, was a valiant heart and unswerving loyalty to the cause.

Chapter 7

IN August 1942, plans for a new form of escape 'through the gate' were being formulated by Grimson and Morris with the backing of Alexander and other members of the Committee. "The Game's good these days, isn't it?" Grimson wrote home at this period to his brother John. "I reckon I'll see you soon. Lots of Luck. . . ."

Later in August, as those plans were maturing, George wrote again to his mother, thanking her for a parcel he had just received, although posted in the previous March. "I am receiving your letters regularly now," he wrote, "but you must not mind if I do not write regularly now as I do not get many letter cards. I have been busy like you the last week and have just finished distempering and papering the barrack room. It was quite a job for it holds twenty chaps."

The 'distempering and papering job' was in fact the construction of a false wall in the barrack room, behind which it was possible to secrete escape equipment and clothing.

Soon after this George made his first lone escape attempt from Sagan. His work with the German corporal in charge of stores had given him the idea of an impersonation escape, because he had noticed that the German was very like him. After they had worked together for some time, he 'acquired' the corporal's pay book and camp pass. These he brought into camp and passed to Sergeant Stan Harrison, who was chief of the forgery department. Quickly complete copies of the documents were made and the originals then returned to their owner. The signature on the camp pass of 'Peschel, Camp Security Officer', delighted George more than anything.

In summer the Germans wore an off-white fatigue tunic and the escapers' tailor, Sergeant Len Burroughs, produced one from the issue German towels which were in fact more like tea towels. Other workers included Sergeant Buffy James, the rear gunner who bailed out of the burning Hampden piloted by Sergeant Hannah, VC. He produced German badges of rank, a leather belt and a pistol holster made of cardboard and stained brown with boot polish. A converted RAF side-cap and a pair of ordinary service trousers completed the disguise. Underneath his military garb George wore a camp-made civilian coat (Len Burroughs' work again).

Jock Alexander and his team worked strictly on a 'need to know' basis – that is, only those concerned were told. Thus few besides themselves were around to watch tensely as George put on the disguise and walked to the compound gate carrying a large German jam tin converted into a bucket. This contained a few scrubbing brushes and cloths covering his escape food and a civilian cap which had also been made in the camp. The corporal he was impersonating was away for the day.

The sentry opened the gate as George reached it, scarcely looking at his papers. Then the watchers saw George walk across the outer compound which contained the sick quarters and camp store rooms and disappear towards the outer gate leading to the German-occupied *Vorlager*.

Things began well for George. At the outer gate no words were exchanged, although George could by now have managed a conversation in German. The sentry took a cursory look at his pass, unlocked the gate, let him through and then resumed his bored pacing.

Now was the difficult time. George had six hours to wait until darkness. His pass would not allow him out of the main gate and George was only too aware that in any military establishment in England or in Germany eagle-eyed senior NCOs were eternally on the look-out for someone idling around with nothing apparent to do.

His first hiding place was one of the lavatories and from there he slipped into an empty air raid shelter. Even George's iron nerves found the waiting 'rather trying'. At last darkness came and he left quietly through the wicket gate at the side of the German officers' Mess, slipping into the woods to change into his civilian disguise.

Now he made straight for the railway station. Nonchalantly he handed in his papers at control. There was no difficulty there, nor at the office where he took a ticket for the first point on his route to the Swiss border and hopefully, across into neutral territory.

At the next step, unhappily, he came to grief. Another ticket was required here. Sitting beside the official at control was a small, ferrety-looking man in a leather coat – almost certainly Gestapo. George was debating whether to leave the station and travel part of the way on foot, when his sixth sense told him he was being observed. With instant decision he marched up to the control and presented his papers. Something was wrong – he never did find out just what: the hastily-forged documents were not in order. In a matter of minutes the escape was over.

Back at Sagan, the camp commandant, the late *Oberst* von Lindeiner-Wildau, gave George the usual fourteen days in the cooler, adding characteristic congratulations on a brave attempt to escape.

Out of the cooler, George resumed planning the big joint operation. But first he found time to write a long letter to his mother.

"I'm sorry I have not written for some time but the last month has been a very busy one for me," he told her. "Since I last wrote you I have travelled about 500 miles, been in two other camps and spent a fortnight in the cooler. In fact I've had the time of my life.

"It is good to hear that you and the boys are still well. I myself am as 'fit as a fiddle' and quite happy. You know, time is going so fast it is almost incredible that we have not seen each other for 2½ years. Soon it will be all over and you will have me cluttering up the house again. Believe me it won't be long."

For his next effort Grimson took Alan Morris as partner. Documents were gained in various underhand ways. Stan Harrison's forgery department was now working all out and Len Burroughs was tailoring harder than he had ever worked in his life, producing not only civilian clothes, but two complete German uniforms to go over the top of them.

The time chosen for the escape was in the week after Christmas when shows were put on in the camp theatre. Incidentally, one of the theatre company, Roy Dotrice, a young Regular NCO, actually started his pathway to stardom in those prison camp performances.

Both Grimson and Morris had noticed that they had near-doubles serving as *Gefreiter* in the German guard company. It was these men they planned to impersonate.

Theatre shows were always visited by the German staff and even rehearsals came under the sharp eye of *Feldwebel* Schultze, the chief ferret. Schultze was a *real* soldier. Badly wounded as a parachutist in Crete, he respected his captives as they respected him. He viewed the job of jailer with great distaste and made no secret of it, but he always did his duty. He was also incorruptible.

By this time the 'duty pilot' system had been initiated. Whenever Schultze or any of his minions came into the camp, everyone who was engaged in anything illicit got it under cover as quickly as possible. The 'pilot' also had the job of discreetly following Schultze or any of his men. It was often necessary to delay the Germans as much as possible, so other Kriegies were nominated to hold them in conversation, ranging from Tony Hunter's aggressive "Deutschland Kaput and upya" (arresting him and marching him off always took quite a bit of their time) to the more intellectual approaches of our German speakers.

Against the somewhat frenzied background tailors, forgers, map makers and plain robbers worked for a hectic nine weeks to prepare the way out for Grimson and Morris. Meanwhile the two protagonists stayed discreetly in the background; for by now both were marked men to the Germans, since Morris had already made escape attempts at other camps. As the night for action approached, Jock Alexander heard that the two *Gefreiter* Grimson and Morris proposed to impersonate would be our guests in the theatre that same evening.

The show opened on Christmas Day with the Commandant and some of his officers as guests. It was a roaring success, for the surprise of the show was a well-drilled chorus coached by a onetime chorus boy, later an

NCO with 34 bombing operations to his credit. In a camp starved of women, the sudden appearance of a line of high-kicking, big-breasted and lightly-clad 'girls' was devastating. The applause was so loud that Stan Parrish's orchestra was drowned, and the chorus lost the step until they could hear the music again. No matter that the breasts were all false or that one of the chorus had all-too-revealing trouble with his panties: the Germans were as tickled by the show as we were, so that applications from the 'other side' for seats increased. This was all to the good.

For three nights George Grimson and Alan Morris dressed in their German uniforms, collected their escape kit and waited, hidden in a convenient barrack, for the word that would send them out into the brittle hostility of wartime Germany. For things were changing now. Night after night our leader 'Butch' Harris was giving German towns and factories the hammer. In the newspapers we had graduated from *Kriegsgefangener* to *Terrorflieger* and *Luftgangster*.

On the third night things began to happen. The two *Gefreiter* were spotted in the party entering the gate. Their presence in the theatre was confirmed and at eight o'clock Grimson and Morris, dressed in German uniforms, presented themselves at the camp gate. They explained they had had to leave early for reasons of duty, and that in any case they didn't much care for such 'decadent' entertainment.

Jock Alexander had the toughest job of all. He had to stay and watch the operation go through. "The theatre party was essential to the operation," he wrote later, "because normally no Germans were in the camp after six pm."

He is laconic about the stress of the situation, but it was there all the same, for he was as much part of this operation as anyone in the camp. In the theatre Jimmy Deans, knowing what was going on outside, was also feeling the strain as he talked and joked with the German officers who were his guests for the show.

"I watched Grimson and Morris pass through the two gates, at both of which they were checked," says Alexander. "They simply had to say something to the guards, with the potential threat of machine guns just fifty yards from them."

Jock was not to know until later that at the first gate the sentry was some yards away. They waited for him and then, as they produced their passes, 'tore him off a strip' for not being at his post. The sentry was full of apologies, unlocked the gate and let them through.

But at the second barrier there was need of very quick thinking. Unknown to them the German security officer had introduced a system of issuing numbers for everyone entering the camp. Accordingly they were asked for their numbers when they presented their passes. All they could do was try more cursing and raving at the sentry for keeping them waiting.

Overwhelmed, he unlocked the gate, froze to attention and let them through.

Again the wicket beside the German Officers' Mess, despite its dangers, was their gate to freedom and the nearby woods. From these they soon emerged disguised as foreign workers, walked quietly to Sagan station and caught the train they had scheduled. It looked as if Jock Alexander's careful staff work and planning had paid off.

But luck was against them. Says Jock Alexander: "They had escaped and despite the fact that the Germans were on their trail within an hour, a witness to the eternal vigilance of the German defence staff on escape matters, they got nearly to Leipzig before being caught by a suspicious railway policeman."

Many ex-prisoners will remember that night. This was an escape that caught their imagination by its skill and daring. No dreary tunnel digging, which so many had tried, but a cool, calm, gutsy walk straight out through the gates to the strains of *Land of Hope and Glory*. For that is what was being sung in the theatre. Under the Geneva Convention national anthems were banned. Instead we sang *Land of Hope and Glory* – and how we sang that night. Even if the clever and knowledgeable *Oberst* von Lindeiner, who had been military attaché in London in 1912, did guess that this splendid work meant more to us than our rather dreary National Anthem, he did not disclose it.

From now on it was a job to curb the restless spirits inside the wires. Even though Grimson and Morris were in the cooler, they had lit a great fire of interest and hope. The hundred per cent support that had been sought by the Escape Committee all those dreary months was coming now. We had won a victory over the enemy – not a complete victory, but one small battle with all the odds against us. After this it was easier to stop private trading between individuals and Germans; most was done through the able Nat Leaman and his organisation. Any special benefits that accrued, like eggs, other extra food or milk, were sent to the hospital for the use of the patients there. It was a good and equitable system.

What is more – and Cyril Aynsley was quick to remark this recently – it showed that we had established a disciplined and working democracy right in the heart of Hitler's Nazi Germany, where even brave and decent German servicemen went in fear of their own political police.

Chapter 8

THE next attempt, a desperate one demanding the highest courage, was proposed to the Escape Committee by Sergeants Flockhart and Chandler. Their plan was simple and dangerous: to crawl across 200 yards of perfectly flat sandy ground with no cover at all, regularly swept by searchlights and under cover of the machine guns in the goon boxes. Then they would make their way into the equally bare warning area and cut through the outer wire.

Grimson, Alexander and Morris found the scheme brave but foolhardy. Flockhart and Chandler were not easy types to dissuade however. In face of their determination, the Escape Committee could only consent, give all the help available, and on the night, sweat it out and wait for what they thought would be the inevitable burst of gunfire.

That night came. Faces blackened, Flockhart and Chandler slipped away into the shadows. The helpers sat in their rooms gloomily awaiting the fireworks. But none came – in fact, the attempt ended in anti-climax. Flockhart and his partner were caught halfway across the compound by the roving dog patrol which the enemy had now introduced into the camp. Fortunately the patrol guards were decent Germans and did not shoot. The two would-be escapers were marched off to the cooler. Nevertheless, as Jock Alexander says, "Such failures were always successes inasmuch as they made camp morale and pride soar and inevitably shook the Germans."

He was right. On paper escape *was* impossible. The German mind could not conceive that men would attempt the impossible: apart from the problem of escape from the camp itself, there followed the even more difficult business of travelling hundreds – in some cases a thousand – miles through territory swarming with people on the lookout for you. Even in the occupied countries the fugitive was not safe. He might be picked up by some helper if he was lucky, but wherever he was on the run, he had to assume that all hands were against him. There were more than sufficient Quislings and other traitors to justify such scepticism. That is why being on the run was such a terrifying, lonely existence. Poland might be the one exception. There the escaper's view generally was that 'if they can't help you, at least they won't turn you in'.

Although Paddy Flockhart was unlucky to get caught this time, it was not the end for him. He was eventually to be one of the escapers to reach England along the Grimson Line

An attempt like that of Flockhart and Chandler, even though unsuccessful, was bound to initiate new pressure from the through-the-wire school of thought. The next people to approach Grimson, Alexander and Morris, now recognised as the core of escape spirit in the camp, were Sergeants Saxton and Joyce. After the near-success of the earlier effort, it was impossible for the Escape Committee to veto their plan, which was largely the same as Flockhart's.

The usual preparations were made. Came the night, there were the quick handshakes, the whispered "Good Luck – see you in London", and they were away. Anxiously the Escape Committee waited. This time the worst fears were justified. They were discovered almost immediately after starting on their long crawl and pinned down by murderous bursts of machine gun fire from the watch towers.

With the Germans in that mood, it was no good expecting the normal rules of war to apply or that two men standing with their hands up would be considered as having surrendered. They just made better targets.

The inevitable German pandemonium broke out. Loud shouting was followed by the tramp of jack-booted feet and a heavily-armed guard company strode into the camp as if they were about to take on half the British Army and not a pair of unarmed men lying dead or wounded on the ground.

By some miracle Saxton was unhurt, but Joyce was wounded. Saxton was marched off to the guardhouse where Grimson, through his contacts, was able to discover what had happened.

It had been sheer bad luck. A sentry rather brighter than the rest swept the searchlight over the open ground just as they started to cross it. He at once opened fire, and at least two other sentries joined in.

Joyce was taken to the camp hospital, primitive as it was. Clearly he was wounded and badly, for his condition grew worse. At length he was taken off to the German hospital and we still hoped for him. That sybarite Ron Mogg, who had received a Li-Lo bed from home, was approached by Grimson with news that Joyce was in great pain and lying in a hospital bed as uncomfortable as ours. The air bed was duly sent and we still hoped. But after lingering some weeks, the gallant Joyce joined the other airmen who, in our terms, had 'got the chop'.

Jock Alexander remembers the camp as 'being a little subdued for a time'. But not for long. As the truth about Joyce's death began to percolate, the mood turned for the first time to really cold anger. We discovered that Joyce had been wounded in the throat. A ricochet had passed through his open mouth without damage to the teeth and had entered the flesh over the spinal column at the back of the throat. An X-ray would have discovered the trouble and the removal of the bullet would at least have given Joyce a fighting chance for life with the odds on his side.

Oberst von Lindeiner was undoubtedly deeply disturbed by the event. He found it difficult to speak calmly of the incident at our regular meetings, when he met representatives from the officers' and NCOs' camps. He did his best to make amends and Joyce was given a proper military funeral attended by his comrades. That was the last time our dead were thus honoured. By then von Lindeiner was already under the suspicion of the Gestapo because he treated the prisoners as human beings and servicemen.

Soon after this, another party of hardened NCO escapers were moved into Sagan from the Schubin camp in Poland, whither they had been banished with 'Wings' Day. Here they had taken part in a successful tunnel escape, though all had been subsequently recaptured.

It came as something of a surprise to George, Jock Alexander and Alan Morris when the Schubin escapers like Sergeants Fancy, Prendergast, Leggatt and Street approached them and bluntly criticised the lack of tunnelling attempts at Sagan. The Schubin men were in fact as tunnel-minded as the Sagan Escape Committee were dedicated to the 'walk-out-of-the-gate' idea.

George's view, and that of his colleagues, was that they had good reasons for not promoting tunnel escapes. First of all, as a small group, they had until recently been kept too busy selling the idea of escape generally. Nevertheless escapes had been organised and casualties had been suffered carrying them out. They had against them a highly active German security staff with intelligent men in key places. Sagan was built on sand and both the digging and the dispersal of soil posed difficult problems.

In the NCOs' camp there was also a certain unwillingness to think in terms of tunnels, mainly because of the unsuccessful attempts made in other camps. Again, unlike Sagan, Schubin was an officers' camp where rank counted and could be thrown behind camp escape organisation. The independence of the NCOs' camps, where many of the men still sturdily maintained their recently and voluntarily relinquished civilian status, had been a problem which James Deans, like Grimson and the Escape Committee, had been working at for a long time.

This dialogue between the opposing parties had vital results for the future of escaping. Sagan and Schubin protaganists quickly appreciated the other's point of view. Both sides agreed that they were now strong enough to mount both kinds of escape, provided the full co-operation of the camp could be obtained. No one really doubted that the potential was there. It was just a matter of bringing into action on the side of the escapers that high spirit of comradeship and discipline which the air war had fostered.

It was agreed that the important thing was to go on showing results, because the bravery of the men involved in escape had already begun to convert the doubters and breed a keener appreciation of what was required from everyone in the camp. Meanwhile the Tally-Ho Club would be enlarged and improved. At the same time everyone would be impressed with the fact that there was still a war on.

"You are still members of the Royal Air Force, the finest Service," the word went round. "It is your duty to escape and to help others to escape. You must be prepared to do anything towards that end. Remember that every escape attempt ties up more troops looking for us and in the end they will have to increase the number guarding us. Any one of those troops could be serving at the front."

With humour and insistence the message was hammered home. The news readers were roped in too. After they had finished the bulletin, they inevitably came up with requests for various items like bed-boards for tunnels or other bits of escape gimmickry.

A response was soon forthcoming. Much undiscovered talent came to the surface and was quickly utilised in the support groups, tailoring, forging and map and instrument making. Tally-Ho went from strength to strength. Escape attempts were planned on a new, broad front.

Sergeant Prendergast was appointed tunnel leader and soon, with his drive behind the project, excavations were under way again. The Tally-Ho Club provided the equipment and supplied the duty pilot watch system. Unfortunately, Prendy's first major tunnel failed owing to a dangerous cave-in when it was halfway to the fence.

Meanwhile the former Dorset farmer, David Westmacott, now in Rhodesia, and South African Buck Easton started a 'moler', or shallow, quickly dug tunnel to the wire. Its start was in a lettuce bed, where David had decided to try to make the sand of Sagan yield something edible. The entrance to the tunnel was covered by a hidden box lid supporting growing lettuce plants which were exactly in line with the others in the plot. When digging was to begin, a group of Tally-Ho members would gather round, the lid would be lifted and replaced again after the two tunnellers had slipped inside.

But the Germans caught on to this one, probably at night when their dogs picked up the trail of the two 'moles'. Anyway, there came the inevitable day when the German search party moved into the camp and everyone started hiding things. This time, instead of entering a barrack, they marched straight to what was known as 'Dave's Farm', lifted the lid and invited the occupants to present themselves. David came out first, then Buck Easton's red face appeared. "I was only inspecting the drains," he observed nonchalantly to the angry Major Zimmeleit, who was *Lager* officer.

This sally was a rich joke to the watching prisoners, for sanitary arrangements in all prison camps were primitive in the extreme. They consisted of huts built over large pits, into which undivided box seats were inserted, and were generally known as hundred- or fifty-holers depending on size. On the rare occasions on which they were cleaned out, a contraption known as 'Die Machine', drawn by an ox, was employed. Suction was started by firing a cartridge in a funnel-shaped construction on top of the tank. This created a vacuum and suction resulted at the other end of the pipe.

Westmacott and Easton were duly marched off to a now tightly-packed cooler, for the activities of Tally-Ho had excited the displeasure of many Germans. As soon as they were let out again, they went to work on another tunnel, but unfortunately this one was not completed before we moved camp.

George and all the other members of the Escape Committee had an interest in these escapes. But George, like Paddy Flockhart, was very much a loner, and in fact Paddy Flockhart was the next to have a go. This time the effort was more sophisticated than a desperate crawl to the wire.

Early in the year, it had been observed that the party leaving the compound for dental treatment in the *Vorlager* coincided for about three minutes with a party of Germans going to the bath house for showers. There was clearly promise here. All Flockhart had to do was to pass through the first gate as an airman with toothache, then in the dental building switch over to German uniform to join the enemy bath party and march out of the second gate with them.

The observation, planning and preparation for this escape took many weeks of hard work by a great many members of the Tally-Ho Club, but halfway through April all was ready. Flockhart made the switch and got clean away. His absence at the twice daily *Appell* or parades when we were counted was covered by his comrades – the Germans were bad at counting anyway. To add spice to Flockhart's escape, he marched out of the camp with the other Germans singing their favourite, if dreary, song 'Orido, orido, orido, orido, orido o-o-o-o etc'. They always sang this when they marched; it reminded us of the Seven Dwarfs in 'Snow White'.

Paddy deserved better luck outside the wire after the perfect piece of bluff and timing which won his liberty. He was bound for the Swiss border, but he was caught on the third day out after laying-up for the night. Nevertheless, we had won yet another battle. After many vicissitudes, we were at last beginning to beat the German security system and the *Abwehr* were plainly geting worried about it.

Grimson, whose audacity and courage were exceptional in a camp which had its share of exceptional people, was meanwhile preparing another surprise for the Germans. He proposed to disguise himself as a member of

63

the *Abwehr* and march four prisoners out of the compound in broad daylight. Unfortunately, it was impossible to produce the papers and other support gear in time and the attempt came to nothing.

Then the Germans sprang their surprise on us. They suddenly informed us that we were to be transported to a new camp 'especially for NCOs' at Heydekrug, on the shores of the Baltic in what had been Lithuania. Most of the local security forces were unreservedly glad at the prospect of our departure and made no secret of it. 'It will be like a holiday camp', they told us. We'd heard that one before.

Before we departed, Tally-Ho managed to strike back at the enemy in an effective way. Among the guards was that particularly suave and apparently friendly type, previously referred to, *Gefreiter* Günther Wagner. We had done a little trading with him and he had brought in some much-needed radio parts. Wagner approached us with the information that the *Abwehr* knew we were operating a forbidden radio set and fourteen days leave had been promised to the German who discovered any lead to it.

"How about it?" asked Wagner. "Surely we can come to an arrangement? Or else . . ." We didn't like it; but Wagner was playing out of his class.

Bristow and his assistants quickly made up a radio set. The notable thing about it was that it had no valves, but it did contain condensers which had been stolen from the camp telephone system by 'Wings' Day's men at Schubin. In fact it contained all the material we did not need.

The set was duly hidden in the cookhouse. Wagner was informed, bore the good tidings to the chief of *Abwehr*, 'that bastard Peschel', and the raid was carried out. Triumphantly the Germans bore away their trophy to take its place in the escape museum which by now was shaping into quite an interesting place. Wagner went off on his leave fortified by some of our chocolate as evidence of our good feelings towards him. We all hoped he would be well bombed. But in case he wasn't, we prepared the next move.

In the new escape organisation, brains were rapidly replacing brawn as weapons. The *Abwehr* and German camp guard had been penetrated to such an extent that we had been warned Wagner planned a double-cross: a snap raid was to follow his return from leave. Since the daily news had been established, another contact service with England had been developed giving us messages and orders, and it was therefore vital that the radio should be preserved. So on the very night of Wagner's return, the news was taken on the 9 o'clock BBC Service instead of the usual midnight one and the set was dispersed and hidden in various parts of the compound.

At 5am we were rudely awakened by the familiar shouts of "*Appell! Raus! Raus!*" Emerging blearily into the early dawn, we found ourselves under an unusually heavy guard, including troops brought in from elsewhere.

Ferrets led by Wagner now tore John Bristow's end of the hut apart – literally. Bristow, wrapped in a blanket as he hadn't troubled to change out of his pyjamas, surveyed the sacking benevolently. Nothing at all was found. The rest of us kept ourselves amused by whistling the Laurel and Hardy theme as the Germans marched from place to place, or kneeling behind one man while another pushed him over – a joke which always amused the Germans.

There was another joke which they did not find so entertaining. A German guard would be engaged in conversation. As he invariably carried his rifle in the slung position with the spout upwards, it was comparatively simple for an accomplice to slip behind him and place a partially-smoked 'Polskie', or Polish cigarette, in the muzzle of the rifle. 'Polskies' had a long cardboard tube at the end and were ideal for the purpose. Someone then drew the attention of other guards to the phenomenon. Since most of them were a rather scabby shower who had no objection to seeing their own people in trouble, they always cackled. What they never realised was that the same thing was being done to them.

Comic opera would then be played *accelerando*. First to storm up in fits would be the *Feldwebel*, followed by a ranting *Oberfeldwebel*, followed in turn by any spare German officers. The sentry and his friends were invariably booked, to the distasteful accompaniment of abuse, kicking and face-slapping which characterised the smoking of this particular 'cigar'. It was all very good for our morale, but very, very bad for the Germans.

The Escape Committee now devised their own special plans for *Gefreiter* Günther Wagner. Although nothing was found in the search, he was soon back in the camp, bright and breezy as ever. "Someone else thought they could get fourteen days leave," he explained artlessly. He even hinted that he might be on his way to *Feldwebel* as a result of his success. He certainly was on his way, but not as he fancied.

Later, when things had quietened down, Wagner returned to his usual bit of trading in the camp. Tally-Ho thereupon dropped word to another *Abwehr* man, known to be a Gestapo agent incognito, that Wagner would soon be stepping out of the camp, his pockets stuffed with English cigarettes and chocolates. The Germans promptly organised a reception party at the gate for poor Günther. Watchers saw him grabbed, searched, slapped and marched off. A few days later, he was seen doing duty in one of the posten boxes. What, we asked him guilelessly, was he doing there? "Extra duty," he replied glumly, "until I'm sent to the East Front."

The effectiveness of Tally-Ho was now apparent to all – even the Germans.

Chapter 9

WHILE the excitements of the previous chapter were unfolding, Grimson was busy working out the coolest and most dangerous escape of his career. The turmoil of the move to Heydekrug was to be his cover.

It takes so little time to write the story of an escape, but each one imposed countless man-hours of devoted work on many people to create the clothes, maps, passes and other material to make it possible. Grimson was one who particularly admired the backroom boys. Not for them the glorious moments outside the wire, even if they were all too brief, or the excitement of pitting wits and skill against a vigilant enemy, only the drudgery of preparation in fanatical detail. Their only reward was the thought that, however tedious the job in hand, from sewing to operating the radio, it was all for the cause. If Grimson, Morris, Flockhart and other escapers were the edge of the sword, the support groups were the arm and body that swung it. Probably the men with the greatest tensions to carry were James Deans, the elected camp leader, and Jock Alexander, head of the Escape Committee.

Two men who were working especially hard and skilfully for the new Grimson effort were Sergeants Ron Stewart and Steve Bevin, who could make almost anything from a few tins. This time they were building an ammeter with a large dial and impressive, dangling leads; for the plan Grimson had submitted to the Escape Committee required that he should disguise himself as one of the *Abwehr* ferrets for the job of 'testing' the boundary lights, until he had the opportunity to get over the fence. This he planned to do by dropping his pliers into the danert wire interval of the main fence, then asking the sentry's permission to go down and get them. After that he would request the sentry to let him return on the outside of the wire, rather than climb through the danert and back into the camp. If the sentry agreed, Grimson was away. If he did not, Grimson was back in the camp and still trying. And if the sentry became suspicious, Grimson was probably dead.

This daring plan required a man who could act a part, speak perfect German and look death coldly in the face. Grimson had all these qualities.

"Although the preparations would be exacting and arduous, we knew Grimson's blood was up when he submitted his plan to the Committee," recalls Jock Alexander. "We could do nothing but accept it and get on with the necessary organisation."

It was "'Arry 'Itler's Birthday' again. We had been at Sagan for a year, during which Monty's Eighth Army had knocked the stuffing out of Rommel's lot, while the Italians, whom neither Germans nor English took very seriously, had gone into the bag in their hundreds of thousands. And of course there had been the surrender of von Paulus' Sixth Army at Stalingrad. Now we were on the move to the new camp at Heydekrug.

As the advance party of NCOs was preparing to march out of the compound, German-speaking members of Tally-Ho were on the watch to make sure that all the *Abwehr* ferrets had left the compound in readiness for the great send-off, where they might expect some smart breaks for freedom. After a quick sweep of the camp, the reports began to come in to Jock Alexander: "All clear, goons out." Meantime George was dressing for his latest part.

With a German field-service cap, a set of German overalls, a leather belt and the impressive ammeter with its leads dangling, he looked the very picture of the duty ferret about his work. Slipping out of his hut after the usual quiet cheerios, he strolled through the emptying camp, pausing only to pick up a ladder which had been left for him inside the camp theatre.

It was three o'clock in the afternoon. All was movement and noise outside as the parties assembled ready to go, but chosen Tally-Ho members were carefully watching both Grimson's movements and the situation at the gate, so that they could stage a diversion if any Germans came into the camp.

George always had a jaunty sort of air about him. Now, with the ladder over his shoulder, he marched straight across the middle of the empty parade ground as smartly and coolly as if he had been at home in Uxbridge. Straight to a predetermined spot only ten yards from a machine gun box he went, then shouted to the sentry and crossed over into the warning area.

The anxious watchers waited for a shot. Nothing happened. George set his ladder against the outer wire of the double fence, climbed it, spanned the fences with a short plank, scrambled on to the plank, then started unscrewing one of the perimeter lights, which he 'tested' with his fake ammeter. He screwed the bulb back, had another word with the guard, then passed on to the next bulb for a repeat performance.

Suddenly he was seen to be at desperate risk, for genuine German ferrets were entering the camp. They were immediately intercepted by watching members of Tally-Ho and invited into the barrack for last cups of tea. Goodbye gifts of chocolate and cigarettes were pressed upon them. "We can't carry all this stuff with us," they were urged, "so you may as well have it."

Out on the wire Grimson was having his own difficulties. Twice he was questioned by patrolling guards who seemed suspicious. Twice he had to reassure them that he was looking for a fault in the wiring, making a great show the while with his home-made but professional-looking equipment.

But he got away with it. Then, at 3.25pm, he got his plank bridge across the wire near a sentry box and managed to drop the pliers into the danert wire. As planned, they landed just inside the outer fence.

George called to the guard. Could he, he asked in German, go down on the outside of the wire to retrieve his tools, then walk round the outside of the wire to the gate, so as to get back to work? Yes he could, answered the guard. With deliberate slowness, George climbed down the wire on the 'freedom' side. Cracking a joke with the guard, he retrieved the pliers from the wire. "These bloody Englishmen don't realise the trouble we're at to keep them in," he observed. The guard chuckled and swore.

Grimson moved off down the wire, pausing at each of the two boxes to pass the time of day with the guard. Finally he was out of their line of sight and slipped easily into the green coniferous woods which surrounded Sagan like a dark cloak.

The time was three-thirty and he was on his way again. The watchers and workers of Tally-Ho breathed sighs of relief.

Outside the camp, the advance party for Heydekrug was being counted and generally mucked around by junior German NCOs in the manner common to every service in the world. *Oberst* von Lindeiner addressed us first, referring to us as "his boys". He warned us of the dangers of escape and pleaded with us to be careful. Our lives would be valuable to our country after the war, he emphasised, and I think he was sincere. Many of us had met the *Oberst*, usually en route for the cooler. We always recognised him as a decent man and many would have been happy to have served under him if only his uniform had been the colour of ours. However, we took little heed of this warning. Then the Senior British Officer, Group Captain Macdonald of Wellesley Long Distance Flight fame before the war, was allowed to speak to us. "Don't forget you are all proud members of the Force which saved Britain and which ultimately will win the war," he said.

By now Grimson had found an old hut in the forest and there he hid until dark. Few of the people on farewell parade even knew there was a man out. 'Dixie' Deans, who was naturally in the picture, was putting on a fine show of unconcern. Through the wire in the officers' compound, our old friend 'Wings' Day took off his cap and waved to us. Others, standing on the incinerator inside the compound and at other points of vantage, waved to friends and crew members. *Feldwebel* Schultze, parachutist, had done us the honour of appearing in dress uniform with dirk by his side, his medals and the coveted golden 'Kreta' armband on his smart Luftwaffe number one uniform. We were glad to see Schultze. Not

The wire, the bloody wire. This was an inside fence. The external ones had loops of danert wire between the double fences.

Left: George Grimson, pictured in the early days of his RAF service, on the River at Putney, not far from his home.

Right: Three of the Kriegie 'greats'. Left Wing Commander 'Wings' Day, he never lost his grin even when they chained him to the floor for escaping from a concentration camp. Group Captain Herbert Massey, Senior British Officer at Sagan, and James Deans who made the ideas of Grimson, Morris and Jock Alexander workable.

Below right: 'Sorry to upset the family', writes George characteristically in a first letter home.

Below: A 'Bind' (Kriegie collective noun) of Kriegies. Willy Woods who spent so many unpleasant hours in a hen house while his future was discussed by the Germans is on the extreme right.

Datum 30ᵗʰ September 40

Johny,

Sorry to upset the family but it could
not be helped, this war gets in the way, but I
was comparatively lucky. Look after mother
for me and dont get mixed up in too many
fights. One of us in the cooler at one time is
enough. The best of luck, your brother

Right: Fallingbostel. The boys come out to enjoy the sight of a daylight raid on nearby Hannover by the United States Eighth Air Force. That was a great day. Note the surroundings. Not up to Colditz standards and 90 in a small room.

Above: This was the show that provided the diversion for George Grimson and Alan Morris to walk out of the gate at Sagan. Compère Peter Thomas with members of the chorus . . . all normally tough members of the rugger fifteen.

Right: Time for a haircut, and a dhobi day for some as the washing lines show.

Top left: Familiar scene at Heydekrug and many other NCO and other ranks' camps. The wheels drive small fans to provide forced draft for charcoal fires. Fuel was always desperately short and a little bit of wood had to suffice for many brews.

Bottom left: Bristow's super-radio built to be hidden in a D-type mess tin.

Middle left: On the march. Jimmy Deans drops in for a brew before his epic trip through the lines. Left to **right standing RSM Tom Cameron, Queen's Own Cameron Highlanders, Jimmy Deans, RSM Turner, Royal Warwicks, radio wizard John Bristow and 'Bill' Stan Williams.** Left front row kneeling, another Regular, Sammy Panton . . . our post master.

Below: Hidden in a German loft, John Bristow operates his set, Ron Mogg takes a verbatim note. The sets and copies of the last notes taken . . . an order to the Germans to behave themselves and to the prisoners to stay put . . . **are to be seen at the Royal Air Force Museum, Hendon.**

Above: Rolling home. A liberated Horsche staff car, 30hp blown engine. Driver John Heape, passenger Cyril Aynesley.

Below: Liberation by a patrol of the Queens' under Lieutenant Potts.

only was he a good man, but it was better that he should be out with us rather than poking that long, intelligent nose around the inside of the wire.

Group Captain Macdonald returned to his compound, where he stood near the gate with 'Wings' Day and Group Captain Massey. We were counted once again. There was also an *Appell* inside the camp, where the rear party was also counted. A neat cover-up job was done for George; the figures agreed. At nearby Sagan station an engine tooted. It was time to go.

James Deans gave the orders: "Right turn. By the right, quick march," followed quickly by "Eyes right" as, with arms swinging, we swept past the gate of the officers' compound. The three figures there came to the salute and held it until the last of the column had passed. Then "Eyes front. March at ease". It was a triumphant farewell and a cheer followed us from the officers' compound.

Marching at the rear, I overheard *Hauptmann* Pieber. "These boys really are *Soldaten*," he mused. "Why do they not behave like this when I take camp parades – or for that matter when any of us take them?"

At dusk, Grimson changed into his civilian clothes (until then he might still have had to play the ferret). He took the food, money and other essential escape gear from his tool bag and buried the evidence of his other identity. Then he broke cover and made his way quietly to Sagan railway station, to join the real German civilians on the platform craning their necks to catch a glimpse of us as we were being piled into '40 *hommes, 8 chevaux*'.

We left much later on our way north and east by circuitous branch lines, to spend much of the night in a marshalling yard just outside Berlin listening to the big city getting a pasting. From time to time, descending flak splinters sprinkled the roof and we took it in turn to peer through the high, narrow iron-barred windows at fires burning not so far away. We were jubilant. George was away and here were we with a grandstand seat for a Berlin 'pranging'.

It was even more satisfying that our German guards, occupying the wired-off centre section of the truck, should be manifestly anxious and in some cases definitely windy. It did not seem to strike any of us that a bombing mistake might turn us all, English and German alike, into what was generally known to crews as 'strawberry jam'.

Cheerfully and rather cruelly we asked our guards if any of them had homes in Berlin and were cursed heartily and told to shut up. But above the abuse and mirth which we returned we could hear the hand-machine guns being cocked. The quiet voice of Jimmy Deans broke in. "That's enough, chaps," he warned. "Don't push it too far."

We subsided into a sort of cramped sleep, conscious that the raid was over. Every now and then the guards would sweep the light of a torch over the recumbent mass to see if anyone was busy digging out the side or bottom of the truck. The train rumbled steadily on.

Meantime George was taking it easy in another train. Anticipating that his absence might be discovered, he had decided to take the most unlikely direction: north and east to the Baltic rather than south-east to the Sudeten mountains, where help might be expected from the Czechs. He was on his way to Stettin in the hope of stowing away aboard a Swedish ship.

Meanwhile the party back in the camp was putting the finishing touches to this brilliantly executed escape, probably one of the best-planned of the whole year. Their first task was to destroy the evidence. George had taken the ammeter with him, so there was only the ladder left to show the method which had been used. Since it was always possible to repeat a successful escape, it was essential that this vital piece of evidence should be got out of the way.

This, thought Jock Alexander, as he made preparations for a night sally, might be unpleasant and difficult. In the end there was nothing to it. One of Tally-Ho's silver-tongued German-speakers persuaded a goon that the ladder had been left by one of his staff and they wanted it back in the theatre. He obligingly had it brought back.

Consequently the Germans never did discover how Grimson escaped. This caused great dismay. Blame and counter-blame were testily thrown around wholesale between them when George was captured on his fifth night of freedom while trying to get aboard a Swedish ship.

At both Sagan and at Heydekrug, where the news arrived almost simultaneously, it was definitely one more up to the NCOs. "At Sagan," comments one member of the Escape Committee, "the defeat of the *Abwehr* was very evident in their glum faces. They were clearly getting the stick. One even admitted that they had all been given 'a big cigar to smoke', which was the Luftwaffe equivalent of the RAF's 'being torn off a strip'. As James Deans used to say, 'They were not happy little Germans'."

Despite the news of Grimson's recapture, the NCOs' tails were well up. Under Sergeant Gibson, who had gone with the advance party, tunnelling was started within a day or so of moving into Heydekrug. By the time the main party arrived, three tunnels were already organised, but one had failed due to the energy and impetuousness of the diggers, which invited suspicion and led to detection.

Before the main party left Sagan, there was yet another escape. Sergeants Gilbert and Wilkie had decided to try the 'dental-party-swap' routine employed by Paddy Flockhart earlier. Unfortunately the enterprise was unsuccessful.

In the next few weeks, the majority of the NCOs, including all the escape experts, assembled at Heydekrug, together with the tailors, forgers and all the other ancillary services needed to make escape possible and effective. Once again, in their incredible way, the Jerries had managed to collect in one place the greater part of the NCO talent in Germany, and all the devoted men whose efforts contributed so much to escapes.

John Bristow's radio was installed and working on Day Two of our arrival and by popular request the news readers were busy doing their rounds, usually at lunchtime when the methodical German marched off to eat. Tally-Ho again provided cover for these news-reading operations and the cry of 'goon in block' would send the reader and his verbatim report scurrying quietly to a less dangerous place.

Heydekrug, claimed by the Germans as another 'escape-proof' camp, was on the Memel Peninsula. It seemed to have been an old military barracks, as the large, long rooms were brick-built and whitewashed inside. At each end of the room were two Russian-type, flat-topped brick stoves which burned a minimum of fuel and gave a maximum of heat. I always find it amazing that one of today's 'whizz kids' in the heating industry has not latched on to that one: there's a fortune in the idea. Not only can you cook on these stoves, but in really cold weather you can sleep on them. Those of us who had wintered on the Baltic in Stalag Luft 1, Barth, and knew what it was to have to saw through a completely frozen loaf of black bread, welcomed this more robust construction.

The prisoners were crammed into these buildings, sleeping in three-tier beds with just enough space between them for a man to move. Best of all, the beds were brand new and each had a complete base of bed boards, all cut neatly to just the size for roofing and shoring tunnels. George, who had joined us again after the usual spell in solitary, looked a little thinner and a little grimmer; but he was clearly delighted with Heydekrug. It was a splendid jumping-off base, either for getting away to Sweden or going north or east to join the partisans known to be operating in the vast forests in those directions.

Tunnel number two failed soon after George returned. It really looked as if the German seismographs in the wire were capable of picking up the slightest sounds of digging. However, under the guidance of Paddy Flynn, Garrioch, Fancy, Prendergast and F/Sgt Ash, who had been smuggled into the main party from the officers' camp, the third tunnel continued.

Conditions were frightful and the difficulties much greater than those encountered at Sagan. The water table was at only eight feet and falls were frequent. Added to this the Germans had conceived the idea of running a small steam roller around the warning area, so that any tunneller who did not want to be crushed and entombed had to get out quickly. Tally-Ho, with its duty pilot early warning service, had to be really on its toes.

Though this was the last of the big tunnels, it turned out to be one of

71

the best ever built in Germany. Despite an earlier-than-planned break, it was 145 feet long and the entrance finally selected was perhaps the most ingenious devised by Kriegie wit. There was abundant brawn for the digging and considerable engineering skill available, employed mainly in overcoming the local difficulties of terrain.

The first entrance, or 'trap', selected was through one of the lavatory seats in the *Abort*. Once through, the tunneller found himself precariously balanced on a brick walk-way dividing the two sides of the hundred-holer. He crept along the wall, bent double, to reach the 'Ops room' or 'Chamber' excavated under the adjoining ablutions building which he entered by squeezing through a hole in another underground wall. The hole was made as high as possible, above what was called something even less euphonious than the 'muck level'.

This arrangement was ideal from one point of view. Dispersal of spoil from the tunnel could be made directly into the cesspit beneath the *Abort*. Waste spoil was the biggest headache of all tunnels. Every goon knew that fresh sand or earth anywhere in the compound meant tunnelling, and that a tunnel meant a 'big cigar to smoke' unless they found it quickly.

However, it soon became evident that spoil dispersal into the *Abort* would raise the 'muck level' to the chamber entrance. Even escape-crazy Kriegies did not relish that kind of death. Owing to the high water table at Heydekrug, it was not possible to channel off the effluent, so that tunnel had to go back to the drawing board.

The problem was brilliantly solved. At the end of the *Abort* wash-house building was a small room containing three hot water boilers for 'dhobying' (washing clothes). Though heavy, each boiler readily broke down into three pieces: a large stand incorporating a fire-box; an inner cauldron to hold the water; and an outer insulating shell. A hole, big enough to admit a man, was broken in the concrete under one of the boilers and the chamber constructed beneath it. The boiler was then re-assembled over the hole. It could even be filled with water, the fire lit under it and the water kept on the boil while operations were proceeding beneath. As the tunnel progressed outward towards the wire, air holes were put up and the draught of the boiler fire, drawing fresh air down the tunnel, effectively solved the ventilation problems. Previously, at Sagan, air had been pumped up to the tunnel face through a 'pipeline' of powdered milk tins joined together, the bellows being provided by a kit bag plugged at the end with a circular piece of wood and with a non-return valve made out of an old boot upper. This had given uneven ventilation with pockets of bad air further back from the face. The immense advantage of the boiler-house trap was that it was goon-proof and a digging team could be put down to work day and night without fear of detection.

One difficulty remained to be solved – soil dispersal. Although the *Abort* was in the same long building as the boiler-house and divided from it by the wash-house, there was a very solid wall without a door between the wash-house and the *Abort*. The spoil would therefore have to be carried outside into the open and back into the *Abort* before dispersal, as no doubt some crafty Jerry had foreseen. This risk was not acceptable and the wash-house was too often inspected to knock large holes in the wall.

As with the other problems, an ingenious solution was found. Two small flues had been built in the *Abort* wash-house wall, backing on to each other with a thin division of brick between them. The flue entries, each closed with a tile, were only about eight inches by six inches, and the Jerries must have felt these apertures were too small to encourage any Kriegie devilment. Little did they know.

About a score of eight inch by six inch linen bags were made. These were filled with spoil in the chamber as digging proceeded and the trap was safely closed with a merrily boiling boiler. They were then loaded into kit bags ready for dispersal. At a selected moment, the water in the boiler would be cooled off and the fire drawn. The boiler would then be dismantled and the kit bags hauled up through the hole and dragged through the wash-house to the *Abort* wash-house flue. The small bags were now unloaded, pushed through the hole and emptied into the cesspit. Like this the spoil from two days and nights digging could be dispersed in about half an hour behind the cover of the wash-house complex wall.

There was one obvious loophole – the risk of a goon's sudden appearance upon the scene of dispersal operations. The lively enthusiasm of the Tally-Ho Club was thrown into protecting the tunnel against this danger. Squads were organised for each aspect of the work and with intensive practice the whole dispersal operation could be closed down, including sweeping up tell-tale spillings of spoil and lighting up the boiler, in about two minutes from the warning 'goons up!'

A 'danger area', the periphery of which was just over two minutes' fast walking from the wash-house, was designated. As soon as a German crossed the imaginary line when dispersal was in progress, a network of watchers passed instant word to a 'top-cover' controller, usually Tony Hunter when he was out of the cooler. The controller then judged the safe moment to start closing down.

Other diversionary arrangements were made, but they only had to be used once. It is a strange but undoubted fact that the excitement caused among the prisoners by a big tunnelling organisation nearly always seemed to communicate itself physically to the more intelligent members of the *Abwehr*. So it was with this tunnel. One fine afternoon, the result of 48 hours' digging was being dispersed. Suddenly, the controller spotted the ferret, a *Gefreiter* called Heinze, twenty yards away and making straight for the wash-house. He evidently suspected something was going on and had resorted to the unprecedented ruse of climbing over the wire, thereby fooling the danger area watchers.

'Operation Diversion' went swiftly into action. 'Aussie' Lascelles came roaring round the corner of the wash-house, hotly pursued by another Tally-Ho member, and all eighteen stone of him collided squarely with Heinze. The wretched ferret had barely time to recover from this encounter sufficiently to start the customary shouting match before the trap had been closed and the last suspicion of soil removed. After that the whole of the perimeter was watched during dispersal.

It would be nice to record who it was thought up some of the brighter aspects of this tunnel, but their names are now lost. The ideas may even have been the product of one of the 'Jam Sessions' organised by Tally-Ho and the Escape Committee to solve difficult problems. These consisted of meetings at which each man said the first thing that came into his head in the hope of cross-fertilising someone else's thought.

Since that day bright young executives in commerce have taken some pride in inventing a method they call a 'think tank' to solve such vital questions as 'which way should the fish finger point?'. I can assure them that the 'think-tank' method was used long before to solve conundrums in what was often a matter of life or death.

Chapter 10

JOCK ALEXANDER, George, Alan Morris and James Deans had decided on the basic plan for escape. It called for nothing less than complete infiltration of the German security set-up. The plan could not therefore be put into effect until some practices like private trading with the Germans had been completely stopped. By this time, with the regular arrival of parcels from home and from the Red Cross, and the familiar relaxation of standards as a result of the move, a number of cigarette and chocolate capitalists had been created, threatening 'devaluation'. Grimson saw their supplies as weapons. He and Jock insisted that they should be used as such.

The enemy, who had so long been having guns before chocolate and cigarettes, were highly exploitable. What was more, since the defeats they had suffered in the Desert and in Russia, many Germans were emerging who were not all-out for Hitler.

With a new German staff at Heydekrug and the breaking of old ties, it was feasible that a monopoly trading system controlled by Tally-Ho could be operated. This was an ambition that had long been partly achieved at Sagan. Now was the time to put it rigidly into practice.

It took every ounce of the considerable leadership of James Deans, to bring this off. But bring it off he did with the help of the Tally-Ho Club and his administration staff led by John Heape, most of whom were Tally-Ho members anyhow.

Before long the trading side under the inimitable Nat Leaman was reaping big dividends. Cigarettes, chocolates and other delicacies unobtainable in Germany were changing hands. But they were being traded for the right things – uniforms, badges and other vital aids to escape, as well as parts for the Bristow radio. What is more, the whole operation was being skilfully and centrally controlled.

As at Sagan, of course, there were always difficulties in accomplishing the vast job of bringing 'free' trading to heel. One sprog new boy even went so far as to complain to Jimmy Deans about his 'rights'. For once the normally urbane Jimmy boiled over.

"Rights!" he thundered as if he were on the parade ground at Caterham. "You're wearing the King's uniform. The only bloody right you have is eighteen inches in the ranks! Bloody good men are getting knocked-off every night in the air and others while they are trying to escape. And you talk to me about rights! Get out of my sight!"

Never again was the question of anyone's 'rights', so far as the Royal Air Force was concerned, raised in Jim's hearing. On the other hand, when it was a question of the prisoner getting a right and proper deal from the Germans under the terms of the Geneva Convention, Jimmy Deans could argue his principles with skill and hang on with the tenacity of a bulldog. It is hard to say who respected him most, us or the Germans. By our Allies, the Americans, who now began to arrive in increasing numbers, he was held in equally high esteem. Many have made the journey across the Atlantic to see Jimmy and some of his gang in the years since the war; one of those visitors has since the war become a General in the United States Air Force.

The control of trading also enabled introduction of another useful institution. Called 'Foodacco' it was run with great efficiency by Ron West and Gerry Tipping. It was a barter shop at which prisoners could exchange clothing or food on a cigarette basis. Coinage not being allowed, we had to invent one of our own, so we went on to the Cigarette Standard. Hard-pressed Chancellors of the Exchequer might even take tips from such a simple device, which was a success from the word go. Profits went to the escape organisation for the bribery and corruption of the enemy.

By now it was spring again and work on the tunnel was progressing well. Suddenly we were subjected to a search of terrifying thoroughness, in which camp security were helped by a local Gestapo unit. The motley collection of Gestapo men, dressed in civilian clothes and wearing all sorts of incongruous headgear, seemed a natural for a general piece of mickey-taking, until it was pointed out that the ominous bulge on the right hip of each of these specimens was hardly likely to be a peashooter.

They missed only one thing: the tunnel. True, they got a good haul of maps and compasses, but we managed on our side to acquire a genuine briefcase full of useful documents.

It looked as if honours were pretty even, but in fact the effect of this search on the tunnellers was disastrous. They had already driven the shaft beyond the wire and were eager for an early escape. Now it seemed there might be another search before the tunnel was due to break in a week's time. Naturally the tunnellers wanted to go at once. They insisted with some reason that they could not risk the loss of a job which had entailed so much hardship and sheer effort. The Escape Committee wanted to wait a little longer, but could not disclose its reasons. The intelligence service had reported that a further major search was unlikely, but that organisation could only exist under a cover of complete security, so this information could not be revealed even to dissuade impatient tunnellers. So a vote was taken and the advice of the Escape Committee was turned down.

The tunnel was on. An early break in the open was to be made. More hurried work ensued in the camp, as the support groups made up civilian clothing, maps, ration books and passes to replace some of those taken by the enemy in their recent search.

George was completely against the early break, which his cool brain had assessed as unnecessary. Yet like every other member of the Escape Committee, he was an active helper once the die was cast.

On the night of the break, there was a great change round of places in the camp as the tunnellers made their way to the dispatching point. Dummies were put into beds for a snap count, people slept in other men's beds and holes were driven in the walls dividing the brick barracks, so that a prisoner could be counted in bed in one room and then slip through the disguised hole in the wall to occupy an empty bed on the other side. The whole evening was a fever of activity while Jock and George wrestled with their doubts.

"I could see no alternative," said Jock later. "We wanted the security of ten extra yards to cover. They wanted to go and tension was beginning to build up in the camp. I had seen the same sort of tension build up before and communicate itself to the Germans, with the result that certain loopholes available for escape had been closed."

Fifty men were packed into the shortened tunnel with their escape kits. It was a horrifying experience, for the tunnel had few air holes and there was little air and no escape until the surface had been broken.

The night was clear and without a breath of wind, conditions far from ideal for the escaper who was going to emerge not far from the sentry's beat. Nevertheless the job was on and the last diggers broke surface. "The rush of cold, fresh air when the tunnel was opened told us what we wanted to know and after the terrifying hours we had spent below ground it was more than a reward," said one of the escapers afterwards.

The first man slipped silently away, pressed low to the ground and worked towards the cover of the trees. The second, third and fourth went safely. Hopes really began to rise. But then a guard caught a noise made by one of the escapers as he crawled for cover. The ninth man made it, but the tenth was detected and the remaining 41 were trapped. The Germans now started firing into the hole. Fortunately, because of the angle, all they achieved was to bring down some of the roof and sides. No one was hurt.

In the German quarters panic approached hysteria. One by one the trapped prisoners were brought out and escorted to the cooler, which by this time was so full that they had to put in double beds for prisoners in 'solitary'.

It was ten days before all were recaptured. Several made it to the Baltic coast in Lithuania and were captured while waiting for a fair wind to carry them to Sweden in a boat they had acquired. That rugged old escaper Sergeant Leggatt got as far as Tilsit before a river police official became suspicious and had him arrested. But even if none of the escapers made it, the effect on camp morale was terrific.

In the early morning of the escape, flustered German guards turned us all out on to the parade ground, then marched us back into our barracks again.

Priority need for the Jerry was some idea of how many were out and who they were, so that descriptions could be issued to the police and other natural enemies of the escaper. The Hitler Jugend were also alerted. These proud possessors of junior versions of the ubiquitous uniform were the downfall of many an escaper, since children generally have more highly-developed powers of observation than grown-ups. We did not like them and the general feeling was that it might perhaps have been better to have knocked off a few of them rather than their elders, some of whom had had the advantage of a decent, pre-Schickelgrüber education.

Back at the camp, no sooner did a guard bring in large boxes of identification cards – one to each prisoner with picture and fingerprints – than he was offered a cigarette and a coffee and engaged in conversation. When he turned round the boxes were there, but the cards had vanished. In short order members of the camp administration, who were pretending to help the Germans by organising a room-count, had them in the hands of Tally-Ho. The photos on the cards were smartly steamed off for future use on forged papers, then the cards were torn up and shoved down the nearest lavatory or burned.

Meanwhile a frightened German ferret had been sent down to discover the entrance of the tunnel. He failed to find the way and returned white and shaking. After another fine old shouting match, the Germans substituted an unco-operative Russian prisoner who just stayed down there in the dark. Finally the chief ferret fearfully made his way below.

At last, since the game was clearly up, members of the Tally-Ho Club yielded to German requests, lifted the boiler and cleared the opening. A frightened but grateful German was hauled up, followed by the Russian.

In the barracks all hell was breaking loose. We could hear captives cheering and singing in the cooler and we cheered and sang back. And about this time the balloon really went up, for the German administrative staff, having got everything ready to check the remaining prisoners with their usual plodding thoroughness, discovered that some 500 identity cards were missing. The *Lager* officer, by now a thoroughly lost soul, swelled the general din and happy chaos by running up and down the camp shouting: "Tiefs, all the Englanders are filthy tiefs." No doubt it soothed his Aryan psyche. Most people prepared to take a day's rations out with them, because it looked like being a long day's count before the Germans finally gave up.

Now the Commandant bore down on the scene. A rather unpleasant fellow who had a spike on his walking stick so that he could stick it into the ground and have his hands free to wave about while he shouted, he achieved some semblance of order. Everyone was told to get on their beds for a count. This proved singularly unsuccessful as, what with dummies in bed and the movement from room to room by some rather too ardent cover types, it turned up more prisoners in the camp than were on the ration strength.

"Vy is this?" demanded the Commandant of James Deans, who was quietly controlling the activities of the chaos parties. Politely James expressed his bafflement, too. But that tall laconic Australian, Godfrey Loder, had a solution. "You bastards treat us like flaming animals, so we've started to breed," he informed the Commandant. "Arrest! Arrest!" was the screaming reaction to that, but Godfrey, having delivered his broadside, had merged with the laughing crowd. Even some of the poor down-trodden goons were seen to laugh, until further screams wiped the smiles from their faces. They were called sharply to attention by the *Lager* officer and the Commandant stalked savagely out of the camp 'handing out cigars' to every German in his path. It was not a good day for goons, but a worse one for the Commandant.

The day was a long one. *Appell* after *Appell* was called and the riotously happy prisoners, flushed with the victory their comrades had gained, did not need Tally-Ho to urge them on in various bits of devilry to make counting difficult. For this purpose we were always formed up in files of five, making it particularly easy to cover a blank file. Inside the barrack rooms, the 'sick in bed' slipped through the hidden bolt-holes to be counted two and even three times over. There was no doubt that we really had got the enemy on the run and we were making the best of it. For their part, the Jerries behaved in a slightly dazed manner as if they were living in a nightmare.

This day Tally-Ho had really proved itself. No more whines were heard about monopoly trading. Intelligence and Rackets Departments, under the capable leadership of Morris and Grimson, were accepted. The whole of the escape set-up had been proved as something worthwhile even to the most cynical doubters in the camp.

Hour after hour the Jerries desperately tried to count us. They counted us front, back and sideways and still they could not discover who was in and who was out. Those missing identity cards were a great help and in fact it was many weeks before German security were able to come up with a figure that looked even fairly accurate.

"Why don't you count the legs and divide by two?" gaily suggested

Sergeant Ron West. The Germans preserved an offended silence. Other 'help' came from Cyril Aynsley and members of the admin staff, who led the bemused German counters to even more astronomical figures. "I just thought of a likely number then doubled it," confessed Cyril after the day's events. In the adjoining American compound, our allies were adding to the fun with systematic goon-baiting.

They were still counting us when darkness came and the perimeter lights came on. The searchlights in the towers swept over the waiting prisoners, who by now were singing joyously. 'Salome', 'Bless 'em all', 'I don't want to be an airman' and other unmilitary songs roared out on the Baltic air.

Occasional cheer groups, usually the Canadians, enlivened the intervals with cries of "Good Old Hitler Hock Him!" or "Deutschland Kaput!" "Why don't you silly squarehead bastards pack it in now?" yelled the Americans over the way. Things were shaping up for a slaughter and James Deans and members of Tally-Ho were getting worried.

But it was the Germans themselves who sparked off the next diversion. The ribaldry tailed off into interested silence as six Germans carrying three ordinary ladders marched into the camp. These they proceeded to set on their sides. Two of the ladders were laid parallel and the third one at right-angles to hold the others upright.

"Ve are going to have a sheep count, vun by vun," announced the *Lager* officer to James Deans. Deans called for silence and explained, deadpan, the German plan. Immediately the night was filled with a chorus of baas. The Germans blanched a little, but pulled themselves together and began herding the first flight of prisoners through the pen. Two *Gefreiter* and several spare officers stood at the bottom of the 'sheep pen' marking their score sheets as the counters shouted '*ein*' when each man stepped over the bottom ladder. Several prisoners shouted a few extra "*ein*s" here and there until they were hustled away, but the greatest joke was that the Germans had forgotten to put a guard on the flanks, so that men once counted quickly slipped back and were counted again. This went on for a considerable time until we began to get a bit bored with the game and fell in on the counted side to see what would happen next.

It was unbelievable. The Germans clustered in a circle, rather like an American football team discussing tactics before a play. Every now and then a head would bob up and give us a cursory glance. Some of the more friendly Germans were thoroughly amused now, although they too had been on duty all day and one of them confided in James Deans that something must have gone wrong, because they had twice as many prisoners as they should have. Wisely James kept the information to himself. The situation was potentially dangerous already and the Germans were known for their sudden changes of temperament from the resigned to the ferocious.

Now they were in a corner, there was no saying what might suddenly start the shooting. After more counting, even the Germans were getting tired and just before midnight we were allowed into our barracks.

Next day German tempers were clearly getting shorter. Even so the second *Appell* brought a touch of grim humour. Suddenly a rifle shot rang out. We stood fast, as ordered, but furtively swivelled our eyes to see who had copped it. In the postern boxes high above the wire fence, the sentries ostentatiously cocked their Spandaus and trained them on us.

Gradually the situation sorted itself out. One of the guards in the compound with his rifle slung had been fiddling with his trigger because he was bored and had inadvertently fired his rifle. The usual ritual of face-slapping followed and the man was marched off. But clearly the Germans were "on the twitch", as Buggy Brims described it, if they were coming in with one up the spout.

A day or so later, one of our favourite, but most dangerous ferrets, Tripanzee, began to take a photograph of every one in the camp to replace the stolen identity card pictures. Tripanzee was dangerous because he spoke English with a pronounced cockney accent, having lived and worked in London for thirty years before returning to the Fatherland. This meant that he could enter a barrack and strike up a conversation with a prisoner and his presence could easily go undetected, unless Tally-Ho was particularly on the ball. Fortunately they were. Tripanzee was one of the ferrets who was allotted a special cover as soon as he entered the camp.

On this occasion, his photography did not prove too successful. Not only did the photographed men give false names and numbers, but Tripanzee was unwise enough to let a friendly prisoner handle his camera on the second day. While Tripanzee extolled the merits of the all-German-made Leica, the prisoner, whose name should have been recorded for history but was not, slipped a piece of sticky paper over the splendid lens. Not even the great German Leica can take pictures through a lens cover. Tripanzee did not notice it as he clicked merrily away, though he may perhaps have wondered why the prisoners were so co-operative. When he developed his blank films later, he knew.

A week after this a squad of Gestapo marched in, again to the whistled strains of the 'Laurel and Hardy' theme. This lot meant business. They made few valuable finds, just the odd map or compass here or there, but they left a trail of destruction behind them. One even damaged John Bristow's home-made clock. They also seemed perturbed by the number of ordinary house bricks wrapped in paper, until it was explained that we turned these into bed-warmers by placing them on the communal stoves and then slipping them into our beds. Even the dimmest German could comprehend that. But it took time. Unlike the members of the Luftwaffe, who in the main kept to rigid standards of honesty, these men were thieves and took any food, chocolate or cigarettes they discovered lying around.

The real sensation came when they discovered under one man's bed the carefully-preserved bodies of a number of birds. Heydekrug was on one of the main migratory routes and many birds killed or injured themselves by flying into the perimeter lights. Their bodies usually fell inside the wire, where they were collected by a prisoner who was a keen ornithologist. He had gathered the little corpses and was preserving them to try a little taxidermy to pass the time. This too was explained, but clearly not believed by the Gestapo who obviously felt that we were so hungry that we were living on bird stew. Momentarily they even looked pleased. Perhaps the most heartening and at the same time terrifying thing was to see how scared the men of the Luftwaffe and their officers were of this leather-coated gentry.

Eventually the camp settled down to what seemed an anti-climax. But under the surface Grimson was getting the greatest of all schemes planned. This was the establishment of an escape line to the Baltic ports, no less. Safe houses would be set up where a prisoner on the run could lay up and recuperate and an escape terminal would be established at the port of Danzig. Here, it was hoped the escaper could board a Swedish ship and eventually get home.

We had not been long at Heydekrug when we made the acquaintance of Adolf Munkert, a Christian German, who was to play a large part in the Grimson story. It happened that Ron Mogg had had a volume of poems published by Basil Blackwell in England. They had been well received and a copy had been sent to the then Princess Royal, whose son was also a prisoner. In due course a letter of thanks and encouragement was sent to Mogg via St James's Palace. Now there is nothing like *Kultur* or royalty to switch on the Germans. The reply was naturally passed through the censor and for a time Mogg was known as Herr Dichter (Mr Poet) until they discovered some of his other activities. But the outcome of this incident at Sagan was that when we reached Heydekrug Munkert frequently found reason for a little discussion with him and to smoke the odd cigarette over a cup of tea.

The talkative Mogg would chat to anyone, even a German. Munkert became quite friendly with him and made it clear that his heart certainly was not in the war, all of which Mogg reported to 'Dixie' Deans, since he was a member of Tally-Ho as well as belonging to the camp administration. In fact, few people did not have two or even four jobs by the time the Deans, Grimson, Alexander and Morris organisation got going on them. Nat Leaman was duly tipped off, since contact with the Germans and under-cover trading, or plain bribery and corruption, were all aspects of his job.

Even before Nat really got to work on him, Munkert surprised everyone by bringing in a volume of Heinrich Heine's poems with a request that they should be translated.

"But isn't Heine one of the proscribed poets?" asked an astonished Mogg.

"Of course he is," said Munkert, "but isn't your Seigfried Sassoon?"

"Only in Germany," said Mogg, to whom this was a sore point.

"That is what I mean," said Munkert, "these translations could be useful to me when we have lost and I can take up teaching, perhaps."

Here was one for the book, and certainly one for Nat. Already he had had Munkert under watch for some time. At the end of the week, following the incident with the book of verse, Nat Leaman made his report to George Grimson and Alan Morris: "Weak, uncertain, a bit apprehensive, but certainly anti-Hitler. This one could be our man. The one we have been waiting for."

And so it proved. In the end, though, Munkert was to prove himself far from weak. He was to be a key man in the whole Grimson victory.

Shortly after this contact, there took place a ceremony so strange that it is difficult to believe that it could have happened anywhere else but in a prisoner-of-war camp in Nazi Germany. While members of the Tally-Ho Club kept watch outside, Adolf Munkert, a member of the German armed forces, stood bare-headed in the camp barber shop, his right hand on an English Bible. In broken English, he swore allegiance to King George VI of Great Britain and promised to aid members of His Majesty's forces to the best of his ability. Leading members of the Escape Committee, who had promised that Munkert would be 'looked after' when the war ended, witnessed the oath.

Chapter 11

BY now it might be thought that we were rather a solemn lot who did nothing but sit around and plan escapes day and night. In my opinion escape prospered because it went hand in hand with other activity that absorbed the mind.

Eddie Alderton, now a professor in an American university, and a group of lecturers soon had a very fine school running at Heydekrug. He was proud that the British press called it the 'Barbed Wire University', and prouder still after the war when many of his pupils gained degrees with extra-mural grants at the best universities.

The theatre has already been mentioned. Its use intensified as time went on. Frank Hunt and Larry Slattery had a splendid classical orchestra going, while Stan Parrish saw to the big band stuff. The orchestra and its practice groups were also useful for cloaking the sounds of digging and other illicit activities.

Then there was the ordination class, which had to put up with a good deal of leg-pulling. Several members did eventually become ordained, notably the Reverend Norman Hennessey, who had carried out much part-time social work with the deaf and dumb before the war. After release he continued it and on his ordination opened a school for people thus handicapped, with its own church of which he is the incumbent.

In many ways Norman epitomised the other side of camp spirit. He was a determined man, to whom the war was a crusade. When he volunteered for aircrew, he was rejected because he was half an inch too short.

"I went back to work and prayed each day that I might be chosen," said Norman who, as a steel-maker, was in a reserved occupation. "Next time I went up for an interview, I just made it."

Muscular and fast in the small confines of the rear turret, Norman was to have many successes until his aircraft was brought down in the North Sea. His hobby was gymnastics and he gave many displays of acrobatic skill and strength at our theatre shows. The Germans who attended were amazed to learn that he had been rejected for the RAF on physical grounds. So were we. Norman had great strength of character, as will have been deduced already; and it takes a man of great faith to kneel at his bedside each day and say his prayers in a room jam-packed with 89 other prisoners, few of whom shared the strength of his devotion. His prayers were always said in a silent room, for courage of any sort is respected by men at the sharp and dirty end of the battle.

This camp was also a great place for skylarks and sport. David Westmacott, the tunneller, could be seen herding an invisible flock of sheep round the compound. He claimed they were good Dorset Down sheep, for Dave came from those parts and, being belligerently proud of it, regularly spoke the dialect whenever he met anyone else from that spendid shire.

Cricket matches, especially tests between England and Australia, were fought with an intensity that would have put Old Trafford in the shade during a 'War of the Roses' clash. Soccer, too, was played with great verve and vigour. 'Honest Winnie' Wilmore made books on all the matches and almost anything else you liked to bet on – all payments in cigarettes, of course. Well ahead of Britain's ideas in taxation, he surrendered a portion of his winnings to the Escape Committee. The soccer matches would have had the stands roaring and cheering in England, but players did not kiss or hug each other when a goal was scored; these were real men who played because they loved the game. If a player was injured, as one man, the spectators would yell: "Hang him on the wire". Then a substitute would be brought on, another innovation adopted many years later by the FA.

Rugby was played with even greater vigour and was remarkably popular with the Germans, who called it *Blutspiel*, the blood game. They really enthused about it and it is surprising they did not adopt it as they have soccer. At Heydekrug we played one seven-a-side contest, but so many casualties like broken collar bones and ankles began to clutter up the sick bay that Paddy Pollock, rugger enthusiast though he was, had to call a firm halt to the competition.

With the arrival of large numbers of Canadians and Americans, we even took up softball – a kind of baseball. This is essentially a noisy game in which the players and audience talk-up the outfield to keep them up to it. To hear the cultured performance of that great cricket fan, the moustachied and dapper Taylor-Gill, almost made it worth being inside.

All these activities, especially the games, kept men on their toes and as fit as the rations would allow. At the rare times of plenty, when large numbers of Red Cross parcels arrived, we were very fit indeed. This was all to the liking of the Escape Committee. Every escaper stood a one hundred per cent better chance if he was fit and tough and able to endure those hellish times when the rain poured and the chill winds blew and there was no comfort to be had anywhere. The escaper also had to do without sleep for long periods, but nevertheless had to remain mentally and physically alert with an instinctive eye for the main chance. The psychological benefit of these pastimes was therefore twofold. We became fitter and tougher and more resistant to the rigours of escape, while the Germans gradually got the idea that the sport-mad British were at last settling down to wait for the end.

Nothing could have been further from the truth, of course. Behind the façade of sport, the 'attack' section of the camp was getting down to business. Past failures had been carefully analysed. It was clear that exhaustion through lack of food and shelter was the greatest enemy outside the wire. Human ingenuity and a steady infiltration of the enemy's security system would get the escaper out. The problem in George Grimson's mind was what would keep him going once he was out.

Moreover, there was a pressing need to get someone home. Apart from scoring our own victory, the Grimson-Morris-Leaman network had collected some alarming information about Vengeance Weapon No Two, the V2 rockets. From our camp at Heydekrug, way up in the Baltic, we could see vapour trails climbing high into the blue – far higher than aircraft condensation trails. What was more, these went straight up and in those days aircraft didn't. It was now not only our duty to escape, but to get a man back with this and other information which was bound to fit the jig-saw puzzle of intelligence reaching Command from many agencies. Our bit of information might just complete the picture.

"It's worth anything to get home just now," said George. "We don't count. It's what we do for the country that matters. The chips are down now."

If the Germans had known this, they might have been justified in shooting the lot of us there and then. As it was, life went on in a moderately restrained way. Christmas 1943, came and was duly celebrated. New boys arrived with monotonous, verminous regularity. As they stood outside the gate, they were greeted by the inmates with:

Q. "How's the war going?"

A. "It's a piece of cake."

Q. "When's the invasion?"

A. "Theirs or ours?" (An indication that at last someone at home was taking a realistic view of security.)

Q. "Has Jane had it yet?" (A reference to the *Daily Mirror* cartoon character of that name.)

A. "No, but they're all still trying."

When the new boys came in they were all carefully screened by our own people, mostly ex-newspaper men, skilled in the tricks of interview. Anyone who was regarded as suspicious was passed on for another interview with George and his men, for the Jerries were not beyond planting a spy in our midst.

There were several simple guide-lines and one was the prisoner's length of stay at the interrogation centre at Dulag Luft. If he had stayed more than three weeks, he either had something the Jerries wanted and would not talk or else he had collaborated to a greater or lesser extent. We were worried about the latter. The silent ones, and they were practically everyone, had a rough time at the Dulag, for the cells were alternately cooled below freezing point and then brought up to an unbreathable Turkish bath heat. Another trick was to keep prisoners in darkness or else switch on lights at all sorts of times, so that time should have no meaning. All this took a fair period of days. After a spell of this sort of treatment and a long ride in an overcrowded cattle truck, prisoners found it a bit hard to be whisked off and interrogated by their own kind as well. But it really was necessary and most of them took it pretty well.

There was a humorous side to these arrivals too. At the time we had codenamed our equipment 'Monica', 'Mary' or other girls' names and the Jerries must have got wind of it, so the reiterated questions of newcomers regarding Jane's virginity got them puzzled. A puzzled Jerry is a worried Jerry and no Jerry can sit still and do nothing in those circumstances. They evidently launched a campaign to discover something about Jane (they pronounced her 'Chane').

"Who is this Chane you are all talking about?" the *Lager* Officer asked a rather surprised Ron Mogg when he was taking a parade one morning. 'Dixie' Deans, approached more circumspectly, was just as puzzled. Throughout the day, Tally-Ho members reported that their contacts were asking about 'a chain or something'.

"The only chain I know was the one you buggers put on my wrists when I was at Lamsdorf," said Buck Easton who had received this treatment after the Dieppe raid and was still sore about it. Loder, the lanky Australian humourist, suggested it must be a lavatory chain. All in all it was not a satisfactory day for the Germans. But it puzzled us too. Perhaps it was a throwback to a day early in the war when some humourist being interrogated at Dulag Luft had solemnly told the natives about a new aircraft called the 'Huntley and Palmer' with 'Crosse and Blackwell' engines and wing-tip turrets. Suddenly, Jimmy Deans hit on the solution. "It's Jane of the *Daily Mirror*, you stupid clots," he roared. We left the Jerries to go on worrying about Chane – it kept them busy.

We had more serious matters to occupy our minds, however. Information had been received by circuitous routes from an English woman living in Sweden that her husband, a ship's master, was captain of a Swedish vessel using the German Baltic ports. Contact could be made with him at what she described as 'The Parson's House'. This was supposed to be fairly near Heydekrug. Trying to interpret this rather scrappy piece of information, the Escape Committee came up with the solution that it was either a pub in a Baltic port, frequented perhaps by Swedish sailors, or the home of a Swedish cleric engaged in welfare work among his co-nationals in Germany. Whichever way it was, the first link in the escape route which Grimson had now formally proposed was obviously the Parson's House and it had to be found.

While this was being worked out, Tally-Ho staged another of their little surprises for the many people who had done so much behind the scenes. While Jock Alexander was chairing a meeting and showing off various items of German uniform and civilian clothing, the door opened and in walked two uniformed German soldiers. There was a moment's panic until the two guards turned out to be Morris and Grimson in examples of perfect Kriegie tailoring. After the laughter subsided, they took off their caps and sat down to talk about the big new effort. Not many details were revealed of course, for we always worked on the 'need to know' basis, so that a chance word or intensive interrogation could not be completely disastrous. All the same it was felt that those who were doing so much of the background work should know something of the design for which we were mutually striving.

The surprise of the meeting was a rifle, a wooden one beautifully carved by Sergeant Webster, which actually had a working bolt so that it could be cleared for inspection. This was the normal procedure when the guards left the compound after counting. The rifle, made out of bed-boards, looked so real that a Tally-Ho leader when asked to hide it in his loft refused, explaining that possession of a weapon would result in a court martial and an automatic death sentence if it were found by the enemy. He was completely taken aback when it was taken to pieces, section by section, and he discovered that it was made of skilfully carved bed-boards.

By this time enemy security had been broken. Nat Leaman's work on Adolph Munkert, backed up by the efforts of Grimson and other members of the organisation, had achieved amazing results. Not only was Munkert supplying us with detailed information on the activities of the guards and conditions in the surrounding countryside; he was ready to act as courier for anyone who escaped and wanted to send messages back into the camp. It goes without saying that he also saw to the supply of German uniforms and insignia as well as civilian clothes.

Another unexpected helper had turned up too. One of the guards, Sommers, was supposedly a *Volk Deutsche*, or 'second-class' German of mixed German and Polish parentage, but in fact he was a Pole and a member of the Polish Resistance. Tragically, the whole of the Grimson underground movement was eventually to founder on the rock of this brave young man, who made the classic mistake of belonging to two covert organisations at once. But at this time he was a valuable aid, a constant source of supply of all the things needed to back up not just one escape, but a whole series.

Hereabouts Heydekrug was shaken by a near-tragedy. Any serviceman of practically any nation who has served overseas is familiar with the letter of rejection from a wife or girl friend who cannot stand the separation. The American services know them as 'Dear Johns' and through the influence of American films most younger Englishmen in the Second World War adopted the same term. In the old peacetime Air Force, however, they were called 'Mespots'. Between the wars, among other unpleasant places the RAF policed was the torrid and turbulent area known as Mesopotamia, or 'Mespot' for short, to which one was posted for five years without a break. It was the practice in the RAF to pin a 'Mespot' to the notice board, so that the recipient would not feel alone in his trouble – a remarkably sound piece of psychology, originated by the troops themselves, which usually worked wonders. We copied it in our prison camps.

Some of the letters were incredible. "Dear . . .", wrote one frail wife, for example, "I have just had a baby by a Canadian officer. Mother has forgiven all. I hope you will."

But there was one case at Heydekrug in which the usual cure did not work. It came to a head one lunch time, when the camp was drowsing. Jimmy Deans was taking his normal daily walk round the camp with Ron Mogg. He always chose this time because he could get a bit of exercise without anyone waylaying him for a chat or a request for solution of the sort of personal problem people were always bringing to him. By a sort of mutual understanding, he was usually left alone for this daily perambulation with Mogg.

Suddenly a man who had just pinned a 'Mespot' to the camp notice-board scampered, shouting wildly, out to the warning fence, hurdled it and ran blindly on to the main fence. Jimmy pushed Mogg out of the way and hurried after the man: "For Christ's sake keep anyone else from crowding round," he shouted over his shoulder, "or they'll shoot. I just might be able to do it on my own."

Hopefully bawling a warning to the sentry in the box, Jimmy stepped across the warning barrier, then strode on to the demented man clinging to the main fence. He knew the guns were on him, but ignored them as he coaxed the wretched fellow off the main wire and back to the warning wire. All Jimmy could do was trade on the fact that the Germans knew him too well to shoot him – a gamble few of the rest of us in the camp would have cared to make.

Mogg kept the crowd from gathering, and soon Jimmy Deans was gently persuading the now quietened man back behind the wire. There he was handed over to Doctor Paddy Pollock who, like Forrest-Hay, was always there when things were wanted of him; and Paddy led the man away to sick quarters. Jimmy looked around. "Come on," he said quickly to Mogg, "let's carry on with our walk. You'll get a *Kartoffel* (potato) gut if you don't have some exercise."

Not a word did he say about the incredible piece of heroism we had just witnessed. Ron Mogg remarked afterwards that while it was all happening he himself was too worried about Jimmy getting shot to be jittery, that came later. "I walked round that bloody compound shaking like an animated jelly," he remembers, "yet all Jim would talk about was some special scheme of his for getting the camp laundering done by a proper laundry party."

"He's like that," said George Grimson later the same day, when Ron Mogg was telling him about it, "if he doesn't want anything said, you've just got to shut up." And to this day Jimmy Deans never talks about it. It was simply one of the duties that fell to him; it needed to be done; it was done and that was that.

Important things were brewing inside Luft VI to prepare for the great escape route, but first Grimson had to locate the Parson's House. Munkert was therefore sent to Memel, where he spent his leave with instructions to locate it, but in spite of several visits and many enquiries he came back reporting failure.

This had George really frustrated, as he had been waiting months for this vital information. Eventually he and the Escape Committee concluded that someone would have to go out from the camp and lay down the escape line himself. Then through Munkert he could report back to the camp that the system was ready to receive more men on the run. George naturally volunteered for this supremely dangerous job – indeed, there was no man more suitable for it.

The situation had been somewhat improved by an intimation from Sommers that the Polish Underground was ready to co-operate and willing to help shelter men on the run, but all this had to be checked. So the Escape Committee decided to send Grimson first to a house recommended by Sommers. From there he was to visit all the Baltic ports within reasonable distance, until he found the Parson's House. If he failed in this mission, he was to keep on trying to establish a route home via one of the ports. Regular contact was to be kept with the Escape Committee through letters delivered by Munkert. These would be perfectly ordinary letters on the surface; even Munkert would not be aware that they embodied important messages in cipher. The object of the whole operation was to establish a regular underground route along which a steady stream of prisoners could be passed into neutral territory and home.

By January 1944, while all Europe was starting to work up a tension for the Second Front which had to come that year, all was ready to launch the escape route, except that a method had to be found to get Grimson safely out of the camp. "What we wanted was a plan which did not depend to a large extent on luck," said Jock Alexander. In the previous year many single escapes had been attempted by hiding in vehicles, under them or in every conceivable place about them. All had failed despite persistent efforts by McConnell, 'Corky' Cawkwell, Bunce and the ebullient Canadian, 'Red' Gordon. Jock had considered these attempts brave but rather crude and therefore ones to which the Committee could not afford to devote too much attention.

Now the perfect method seemed to be emerging and it looked as if it might be the first of a series which would utterly baffle the Jerries. Through our close contact now developed with the Poles, it was agreed that George should be taken out of the camp inside the inverted box which served as a seat for the Polish driver of a horse and cart paying regular visits to the camp. By this time George could speak perfect colloquial German and would certainly pass anywhere in captured Poland or in East Prussia. He was also fully equipped with food, passes and other documents.

The day appointed for the escape came: but the wrong driver turned up. Day after day George donned his escape gear and waited, but still our man did not appear. Clearly, this one was not on.

Finally it was decided to repeat a trick which had already been successfully performed by Tubby Dixon at Barth and to go out under the pretext of doing something to the drainage system. This was promising, as a drainage trench had just been dug from the north-east wash-house. It was planned that George, dressed as the German foreman, should walk out that way. But while George was putting on his disguise, the German security officer noticed the site, summed it up as a potential escape route and had the trench filled in.

After that a hectic time ensued for everyone. The Escape Committee had a third plan, requiring a lot of equipment, and proceeded to put it into effect at once. Because of the comparatively mild weather, the afternoon count took place outside on the sports-cum-parade ground. It had been noticed that usually the guards for this parade entered the compound beforehand and took up their allotted positions, which they maintained until dismissed by the *Lager* officer. There were about twenty guards; and when the whistle for the end of parade was blown, they did not form up in military fashion, but slouched off individually through the camp gates into the *Vorlager*.

The *Appell* was held at 3pm, since winter twilight comes early in those Baltic latitudes. It was therefore of great importance that the counting, which normally took no more than 20 minutes to half an hour, should be delayed for at least an hour, if the plan were to succeed. After a briefing by the Escape Committee, Jimmy Deans issued his orders to Ron Mogg, who was to take the parade, and to Hank Heape and Cyril Aynsley who were to 'help' the Germans with their counting. Other Tally-Ho prisoners were warned to be ready to be counted 'sick in bed' and nip through the holes in the wall to the next barrack to be counted again.

The counting went off exactly as prescribed, with three extra counts and a long and acrimonious 'inquest'. It was not over before darkness and the switching on of the perimeter lights. At last the parade was dismissed and the prisoners drifted slowly back to their barracks.

Twenty guards had come in. Twenty-one went out. When the whistle was blown, George had got out of the bed where he had been hiding, slung his beautifully-made dummy rifle on his shoulder, put on his German cap and sauntered across to the gate. He was the third or fourth guard to leave. Since there was no commotion when the last guard went out and the gates were finally locked, he had obviously got away with it so far. Counting never seemed to be the Germans' strong suit.

In the *Vorlager* he went to the lavatory and dismantled the dummy rifle. Then he walked across to the locked hut where the prisoners' spare Red Cross parcels, personal clothing and food were kept. This was the store-room under Alfie Fripp's charge and its key was closely guarded. However, you can't beat a 'Trenchard Brat' and Alfie had had a copy of the key pretty well from Day One on when the store was opened, so George had no difficulty in getting into the hut. Here he hid the rifle in a pre-arranged place and picked up the trilby hat, civilian clothes and a brief-case containing the documents which had been prepared for him. His discarded German uniform he hid for the next man out. The scheme was working.

The date was the 21st January 1944, and for most of us in the camp it was the last time we were to see George. The following day Alfie Fripp and his band of helpers, all undercover Tally-Ho men, bore the packing-case containing the uniform and rifle back into the compound. It had been an immaculately executed operation – so far.

92

Chapter 12

IN the silence of the deserted store, Grimson spent the longest hour of his life. He intended to catch a train at the local station of Heydekrug and travel first to Insterburg, but the train left at 5.45pm and he felt it inadvisable to spend too much time in the vicinity of the railway, which was always a resort of Nazi officialdom. So he waited as the grey Baltic twilight deepened into night, keeping his mind off the dangers to come by rechecking the necessarily complex details of his route.

At that time main-line trains in Germany were always subject to frequent checks by the Gestapo and the men detailed for this duty were some of Himmler's brighter 'whizz-kids'. George therefore proposed to change trains six times, so as to make the 400-mile journey entirely on slow, local connections. He was heading for the village where the family of the guard Sommers lived; from there it was only a few miles to the remote cottage home of Sommers' friend, a Polish forester, which he hoped to make a centre for his operations.

At last the minute hand of Grimson's watch showed that the wait was over and he stealthily left the store, locking the door behind him. Within three minutes he had climbed the single-strand wire fence of the *Vorlager* and was safe in the road beyond. There were few people about as Grimson bent almost double to the Arctic wind and waded briskly through the slush of the previous night's snowstorm.

He had timed it nicely. As he stamped the snow off his boots in the booking office, the train was almost due. At the rail control his good German, well-tailored civilian clothes and perfectly forged passes, gave him no trouble. The security man took only a perfunctory glance at his papers and the ticket clerk cracked a crude joke. "*Schnell* (hurry)", was the only comment from the ticket collector, pointing to the train noisily decelerating into the platform.

George prudently moved towards the end of the platform. It would not do to meet any of his 'friends' returning from leave. The train pulled out and he settled down between two honest burghers in the unheated carriage, lit a cheap cigarette and kept his fingers crossed.

The trip turned out uneventful. None of the many officials who examined his forged papers gave them a second look. In the icy weather few people were talkative or interested in anything but their own affairs.

He arrived late next day and received a warm welcome from the forester and his family.

For several days George rested. The cottage lay deep in the forest, about 90 miles south-east of the Port of Danzig. George could see at once that the area was ideal for an initial reconnaissance of his purpose.

His first job was to write a letter to Munkert, partly to test the courier chain and partly to ask in code for tobacco, cigarettes and chocolate for trading purposes. In due course the letter was delivered by another guard, who had also fallen into the Escape Committee's net. This guard brought an additional and later verbal message when he returned from leave, to say that George was on the move again. He had had to leave the forester's house, because a woman in the family seemed to be talking too much about him to other Poles in the neighbourhood. Rather than risk recapture and the inevitable torture and destruction of the forester's family, including the talkative woman, he had decided to set off on a tour of the Baltic ports. Here he hoped to find the Parson's House, or make some other arrangements to receive the next escaper whom he knew would be due out soon.

For a fortnight the Escape Committee sweated it out and waited for news from George, until their patience snapped. Paddy Flockhart now slipped out of another compound disguised as a civilian foreman. His escape, too, was uneventful and he got off similarly by train for the forester's cottage. The following day, the 19th February, Munkert received a direct request from George to meet him back in the town of Heydekrug.

Munkert told the Escape Committee. After they had deciphered the letter for themselves, they agreed that he should comply and give Grimson a written report of events in the fortnight he had been out of touch, including news of Paddy Flockhart's escape the previous day with instructions to go to the forester's hut. They also sent Grimson a map of the Port of Danzig, which was to be invaluable.

Grimson and Munkert duly met in Heydekrug despite the risk, for it was essential to exchange information. Grimson handed Munkert a written report of his considerable travels in search of the Parson's House. No Swedish ships were trading from Memel, he said, so he had gone to Danzig. Here, in the seamen's quarter of the city, he had eventually found a Swedish parson running a seamen's hostel. At first the cleric denied all knowledge of the Swedish captain George was seeking, but after a good deal of cajolery he eventually allowed George to search the register of Swedish seamen; and there George discovered the name he had been seeking. The man had not been registered there for fifteen years.

Not surprisingly, perhaps, there was an ominous tone of despair in a personal note to a friend in the Escape Committee which Munkert also brought back from Grimson. Despair was the greatest enemy of the escaper. Everyone suffered from it at some time or another. Those fortunate

94

enough never to have been 'on the run' cannot appreciate the loneliness and helplessness which can eat into a poor wretch who feels every hand against him, and is hungry, cold and exhausted to boot – as an escaper almost always is. The POW escaper had to fight despair with every last ounce of willpower, for it made him careless; it weakened his resistance and made a nice warm cell, or almost anything else, seem preferable to the desperate existence he was leading.

In his note George said he had spent the greater part of his time outside the wire catching trains and snatching a few hours' sleep wherever possible in unheated waiting rooms. He was also debilitated by the familiar stomach trouble of the undernourished and overstrained. Characteristically, his greatest worry was that he had been at liberty for over a month with nothing tangible achieved: surely the Escape Committee must be disappointed in him. All he had managed to do was to contact a number of Polish workers and outlaws in Danzig and in areas around the old Free City. Nevertheless he wanted to go on with the plan, so he had arranged to stay at the home of the original forester's brother, who lived in a wood some miles distant from his first bolthole. An innkeeper had given him food coupons in exchange for chocolates and cigarettes, but he wanted more supplies, including children's clothing if that was possible. He would collect the supplies from Munkert later.

A postscript, however, showed that the superbly confident Grimson we knew had suddenly revived. Having heard about Flockhart, he was going back at once to the original 'safe' house, as Paddy might be in difficulties. About a fortnight later, a message came through reporting laconically that Grimson had contacted Flockhart and got him aboard a Swedish ship.

There was, of course, much more to the affair than that brief communiqué. When he first made contact with Flockhart, at the second 'safe' house, George had had to tell Paddy that he had not succeeded in arranging a ship passage, but he thought it should not be difficult to board a Swedish boat in Danzig Harbour. They decided to travel to Danzig that same day. After a few hours' sleep, they set off taking different routes because they had identical documents, and at ten o'clock that night they made their rendezvous in Danzig railway station. George, who by that time was familiar with the dock area, led Paddy to within a short distance of a Swedish ship which was being loaded. Paddy handed George his briefcase and forged documents, arranged to meet him at the station waiting room at dawn if things went wrong, and set off for the last hurdle of the escape course.

While an anxious George walked back into the city, Paddy slipped into the prohibited dock area through an open gate and managed to crawl through the snow to a spot close to the far too well-lit quay side. After watching for four hours, he shifted his position to conceal himself behind

95

a train standing 30 feet from the quay side. Then some German workmen arrived with a railway engine, and Paddy decided ruefully that this was not his night. Disconsolately, he made his way back to the railway station where George was still waiting as promised. George told him that the nightly examination of identity papers had taken place some time previously, so they could spend the rest of the night in the waiting room.

Next day they mooted boarding one of the ships anchored off-shore. George suggested that he should look for an unattended boat to 'knock off', while Flockhart toured nearby Gdynia to see if there were any Swedish ships there.

George scoured the port area unsuccessfully for a rowing boat, meantime Paddy got a nasty surprise on his errand. He quickly found that Gdynia was a heavily-guarded German naval base without a single merchant ship in it. George had had some success, however, as he had spotted another Swedish ship in a different part of Danzig harbour. It looked as though it could be reached through a hole in the quay fence close to an anti-aircraft battery.

After dark, George led Paddy to the hole in the fence, took his papers and walked off. Paddy crouched in the snow until the coast was clear, crawled to the fence, found the hole and wriggled through it. To his surprise not one but two ships flying the Swedish flag were lying nearby. He chose the larger of the two and began to move towards it, but his intention to board was thwarted by a German guard patrolling the quay, who turned and came straight for him. It looked all up. Mercifully, some Swedish seamen appeared and the guard moved over to examine their papers. Paddy hurried away into the darkness and re-climbed the fence some distance from the hole by which he had entered.

Back at the railway station he saw George, but the other made a cautionary sign and they pretended not to recognise each other. Until early next morning they sat in different parts of the waiting room. Then they felt it safe to come together and Paddy described his experience. Despite his toughness, Paddy was suffering from lack of sleep, but George urged him to try yet again that night. Paddy insisted that he would sooner have a go in daylight if only George could find him a cap with a shiny peak and some workmen's overalls. George said he would try and slipped away. In three hours he was back with the required clothing.

George stood guard outside the station washroom while Paddy cleaned up and changed. After a suitable interval, George knocked on the door, to signify that the coast was clear, and Paddy slipped out, handed George his raincoat and walked to a tram stop. George, following on, paused beside him for a moment, whispered in English, "Good Luck", then went on his way in the darkness.

This time the luck was good. Arriving back in daylight at the hole in the dock fence through which he had passed only the previous night, Paddy found a well-trodden path; it was obviously a popular short-cut. When he crawled through the hole and made his way to the dock road, no one took the slightest notice of him. He then walked across the docks and rail tracks to a small wooden hut, which he had noticed but had been unable to investigate the night before.

From this hut Flockhart reconnoitred the scene carefully. Nearby some Russian prisoners, watched by a bored German guard, were loading the ship and a similar party was busy on a smaller quay. Otherwise little was moving. It was noon and Flockhart felt most conspicuous because every other civilian worker seemed to have disappeared, presumably for lunch. For half an hour he lurked near the Russians, hoping that one might leave the party long enough for him to ask for help in getting aboard. Betrayal was a risk he felt he must now take if necessary. But no Russian came near enough, so Paddy was driven back on his own resources. He slipped back into cover and removed the distinguishing yellow 'P' for Pole from his overalls, then re-approached the ship again and began examining its mooring warps. He was banking on the sentry mistaking him for a member of the crew, which is just what happened. After inspecting the forward warp for a few minutes, Paddy walked back to the gangway and climbed aboard unobserved.

After all the previous frustrations and alarms, it was as easy as that in the end. Once aboard, Paddy hid in a boat on the main deck. The ship sailed at ten in the morning of the 25th February, after being searched by the Germans, the only episode to cost Paddy a few heart-stopping moments. Next day he came out of his cache and proclaimed himself a stowaway. To his relief the captain told him the ship was already in Swedish waters and would arrive next day at Stockholm. They even placed a cabin at his disposal. On arrival, Paddy, soon to be Squadron Leader Flockhart, DCM, was handed over to the Swedish police, who in their turn passed him over to the British Legation. Ten days later he was on his way by air to England.

The first of the Grimson-Alexander escapers had made it. This was victory indeed, but with one small flaw. The Escape Committee and Paddy himself were all relying on his ability to remain in Sweden for a time to set up a firm base from which to work the escape route. This would have been a lot easier than trying to do it from inside a German prison camp or on the run like Grimson. It seems that the Foreign Office in their wisdom saw it differently, but knowing Paddy Flockhart I can imagine that it must have taken the Embassy staff a great deal of effort to keep him from his objective. Anyway back in England Paddy still continued to do good work for his comrades in the bag.

At Heydekrug Jock Alexander hid his disappointment and got on with the job. The next man out was Callender. Our intelligence received information that there were preparations for considerable modifications to one of the camp wash-houses. During the alterations, the building would be wired off from the rest of the camp. Further, it was proposed that access for the repair workers would be through a temporary hole cut in the perimeter wire. As soon as this news came through, the various undercover departments went into feverish activity and Callender was ready for the break a day before the new fence was erected. He was placed in a boiler in the building and left there while the Germans marched their slave workers into the compound to wire off the building. For fifty-six hours he stuck it out and throughout that time members of the Escape Committee took turns to keep ceaseless watch on the building. Jock Alexander and Alan Morris barely slept. Finally, they were rewarded by seeing Callender emerge as a German civilian and make his way through the gap in the fence.

It is unlikely now that anyone will discover what happened to Jock Callender. That he made the rail journey to Danzig without detection seems proven, because he spoke to a Polish underground worker there several days later. He may even have been at large some months after. But then, silence. . . . He made no contact with Grimson and failed to turn up at the safe house in the forest. Most likely he died, probably unpleasantly, at the hands of the Gestapo. No record, however, could be found after the war and all official enquiries were fruitless. Jock remains an honoured name on the roll of prisoner-of-war endeavour.

In the meantime, a letter arrived at the camp from Grimson which indicated that he was in considerable distress. He had travelled the Baltic coast from Lübeck to Memel, searching for the elusive Swedish contact. Both his feet were poisoned through walking in over-large boots and he had body lice through sleeping in wretched hovels. But what worried him most was his failure to find the Swedish captain and get the escape route running perfectly on an organised basis. Paddy Flockhart's arrival at the forester's hut had put the Poles there in such a panic that they would no longer give shelter even to Grimson.

Despite this, George would not give in. He haunted the Danzig docks, all the time recruiting help. He even procured a rowing boat, with which he reconnoitred the harbour. Several times, when he approached French working parties for help, he was betrayed to the Germans, but his sixth sense of the escaper was now well-developed and he had disappeared before the police or the Gestapo could pounce on him. Twenty-seven times his documents were checked by Gestapo officials, and to make matters worse he was caught up in the great search for escapers from the officers' tunnel at Sagan. During one of these blitzes, German police took apart the house which was giving him temporary shelter, and George had to spend six hours up to his waist in the snow outside, wearing only his shirt.

With his knowledge of Danzig, it would have been comparatively easy for him to jump a Swedish ship and make off to England. But he had a self-imposed duty to other prisoners of war on the run, so he remained on the job, hiding and eating when and where he could. All the time he kept in contact through Munkert, asking for various supplies for bribery and for copies of new passes and documents which needed to be changed frequently.

Meanwhile the German security forces and the Gestapo were taking a much keener interest in RAF prison camps (Schickelgrüber himself was reputed to be involved). The natives displayed their sharper hostility in several ways.

Most of the known escapers were already semi-segregated in A Barrack, a hut at one end of the *Lager*. This arrangement was supposed to make it easier for the Germans to 'control' the escapers by having them all in one place, but in practice it had the opposite effect. It simply congregated all the key men and made it easier for them to plan escapes and devices to undermine German discipline. Moreover, when George went out and stayed out, the Germans never discovered his absence from the special barrack, as his place was taken by another Kriegie who resembled him in build.

However, worse nastiness was to come. Taking parade one morning, Ron Mogg was astonished to get an order that all Jews were to parade separately and be segregated in a single barrack. Naturally he refused to comply and the usual Teutonic hubbub ensued. Mogg was about to tell the Germans to 'get knotted' when a greatly incensed Jimmy Deans arrived. In clipped German, he out-shouted them all; the order, he told them forcefully, would not be passed on. He sharply pointed out that the prisoners were members of the King's Service and it was one of the rules of that Service that the faith of all denominations should be respected – "even bloody tree-worshippers", he added (at the time tree-worshipping and other pagan rites were being actively promoted by Arch-Crackpot Goebbels). The Germans gave in. Anyway, it would have been difficult to order Nat Leaman to segregate himself as he was already segregated in the escapers' hut.

With three escapers out, morale was sky-high, though the camp knew little of their vicissitudes or that only one of them had got home. On the other hand, German morale, what with defeat in the Desert, a series of 'strategic' retreats in the east and constant heavy bombing from England, was, as Bill Williams said, "so low that any Kraut could walk under a snake's belly-button with an umbrella up and not touch it".

Maybe the high spirits accounted for an outbreak of really gross punning around this time. The penalty for making a pun was to be 'donged' – that is, struck sharply on the forehead with the palm of a hard hand. Lionel Hollidge, now a respected civil servant I believe, was the greatest punster of them all, as well as being one of the key figures in the Tally-Ho intelligence system. His finest invention came while we were queueing at the cookhouse for one small piece of tough stewed horse and two potatoes per man. "Ah!" said he, "horse and *Kart-offel*, I presume." (*Kartoffel* is German for potato.)

Inside the camp, the Escape Committee was finding it difficult to hide their stock of escape equipment and food, which by this time was considerable. It was also getting difficult to cover up for all the men who were out. Covering up was less of a problem than it might have been, because the goons seemed almost to have given up counting and tended to rely upon their 'minders', Cyril Aynsley and Hank Heape, for the camp strength. The chief danger was a snap *Appell*, when the finely-organised counting machine might be thrown out of gear by an over-zealous performance from one of the 'invalids' popping through the walls from one bed to another.

Another danger was the increasing interference in camp affairs by the Gestapo and *Kriminalpolizei*, who were now sweeping through the camp on regular searches. These people were an unpleasant lot, but thorough. Nevertheless, the clever carpentry of Frank Redding and Webster, whose false walls and panels were prime pieces of craftsmanship, defeated them again and again.

Besides being thorough, this bunch of thugs were great thieves and would steal any food they found. One young prisoner was so incensed at this that he made up a sandwich of black bread and an unmentionable substance laced with mustard. After the search the sandwich was gone. That night ninety very highly satisfied if slightly nauseated airmen slept happily. Next day the whole camp knew about it, including the German staff, who hated the Gestapo and *Kriminalpolizei* and were not slow to pass on the glad word of their discomfiture. After that there was a great deal less stealing, but a great deal more senseless destruction, especially of books.

None of the Gestapo or *Kriminalpolizei* searches took us by surprise, thanks to the magnificent contact work put in by Nat Leaman and Townsend-Coles. They probably knew more about these operations than the camp Commandant.

Chapter 13

IN spite of searches and the various alarms, the escapes went on.
Sergeant Lewis went out next through the trench which ran behind
the newly constructed wash-house. He left in the same way as Callender, dressed as a German civilian, and strolled quietly off into the
distance. Watching members of the Tally-Ho Club remember that he put
up a really first-class performance and even seemed to have mastered the
heavy, slightly rolling gait of the German workman. After such a good
start it was unfortunate that he was spotted in fairly short order and brought
back to the camp.

"By now," recalls Jock Alexander, "we had four men out and the
difficulties of concealing their absence were increasing. We decided to let
the total get to six; and then, after warning Grimson, to let the Germans
know we were six men short. This would give the impression that they
had escaped together."

This was sound thinking, for one of the most effective ways of protecting
a prisoner from the evils of the Gestapo was to inform the Protecting Power
of his escape. Unless this was done, the Germans had been known to deny
all knowledge of a recaptured prisoner and could do as they wished with
him, which was plenty. They had, however, an extraordinary respect for
the Protecting Power and would acknowledge, in most cases, that they had
a man when official enquiries were made about him. What is more, the
prisoner was usually returned to the prison camp from which he had
escaped – or at least, he was until Himmler really took over.

By now Grimson had begun to achieve a good deal of success. He had
managed to set up a chain of flats and lodgings which he kept going with
his stocks of food received from Heydekrug. He had decided that prisoners
would be better if they were tucked away in his safe houses until they could
make the attempt to get aboard Swedish ships.

In a letter to the Committee via Munkert, he said that he now had
several Poles working for him and that he had contacts with a number of
foreign workers in the docks. He suggested, therefore, that anyone who
escaped from the camp should make for a place outside Danzig Docks or
the railway station. He intended to hang around the station between noon
and 1pm, and 7.30pm and 8.30pm daily. Anyone who was unable to contact
him there should go to the dock notice-board and make a mark on a
particular ferry timetable to indicate when he would return there. The

notice-board was to be kept under constant observation by one of George's Polish helpers, so that the escaper could be assured someone would be there to meet him when he returned at the hour he had marked.

The next two to go out were a Palestine Jew serving under the name of Jack Gilbert and his friend R. B. H. Townsend-Coles. Their orders from Jock and Alan were to proceed into Lithuania, lie low for a few weeks there while they viewed the general situation, and then make for Danzig and George. They used the Flockhart method, walking out as German civilians.

The escape went off faultlessly. Following their instructions, they made their way towards the Lithuanian border, but when they reached the border at a place near Nowemiasto, about six miles from the camp, they found themselves mired-up in a swamp. After consultation, they decided against pressing on to form a Lithuanian base because of the intense cold and to go straight to Danzig.

They had escaped on 3rd April. Next day George visited Heydekrug to see Munkert and was advised. But Gilbert and Townsend-Coles were already in Danzig and dutifully waited at the station until 7.30pm. By then it was too late to go to the dock notice-board, so they hopefully approached some Poles at a street corner, one of whom agreed to hide them for a day or so. After laying up for two days, they went to the dock notice-board and made the mark specified by George, but there was still no sign of him. In desperation they canvassed several Swedish sailors for help aboard their ship, but in each case unsuccessfully.

Meantime George was hurrying back to make contact with them. As the train carried him through Poland, a disaster which would engulf many people was threatening.

On 12th April, Nat Leaman, the next man selected to use the route, was escorted by Munkert from A compound to an adjoining compound. As head of the trading organisation, he was a fluent German-speaker, and was in possession of the usual forged documents and identity cards. He was to escape dressed as a ferret carrying his gear with him.

By noon he was dressed and waiting in a hut. Tally-Ho took a good look round the camp and gave him the all clear. Nat walked to the gate in the north fence and was safely passed out by the guard, but as he headed towards the sewage farm, the guard unexpectedly shouted after him that he must first book out at the nearby guardroom. Nat replied that he did not think that this was necessary, but the guard was insistent. So, with his mind in a whirl, Nat walked to the guardroom and reported to the sergeant in charge.

The sergeant was inquisitive. To which Company was Nat attached? "Third Company", replied Nat. The sergeant examined the ferret's pass, turned it this way and that, then looked up. "I think you're a prisoner," he said.

For Nat the game was up, but while the Germans phoned for the *Abwehr*, he manoeuvred his way to the guardroom stove and thrust his forged documents into it, burning his hands in the process. Unluckily a member of the *Abwehr* entered the room at that critical moment, took in the situation very quickly and grasped the smouldering documents out of the fire. Sufficient of the papers was salvaged to provide damning evidence, which was also desperately dangerous for Grimson and other escapers who were on the run with similar forgeries. After being searched, Nat was taken to the Security Office for interrogation. Later he was put in the camp cooler, where he was again grilled, not only by members of the security staff, but also by a member of the *Kriminalpolizei*. Things looked very unhealthy for Nat, who was also glumly aware that the balloon was really about to go up for the lot of us this time.

Meanwhile Grimson had arrived back at Heydekrug ignorant of Nat's capture. He was met by Munkert and Sommers, who gave him a letter reporting the circumstances of the arrest earlier in the day. Because his documents were now in all probability compromised, George was advised to get back to Danzig and go to cover for at least two weeks. Grimson in his turn sent in a message to the Escape Committee that he had heard from one of his Polish helpers of the arrival in Danzig of Townsend-Coles and Jack Gilbert. He added that he proposed to return immediately and find them. But, he warned, things were getting increasingly difficult.

Grimson was as good as his word. He went straight back to Danzig – but not to go under cover as he had been urged. On 14th April, Gilbert and Townsend-Coles were exultant when they made their daily visit to the dock notice-board and found a time marked for a later meeting with the initials 'G.G.'

They returned at the stated time, but to their dismay there was no sign of George. After a while they noticed a man watching them. Eventually he approached and spoke to them warily in Polish. It took some minutes before he succeeded in identifying himself to their satisfaction as one of George's helpers. Then he handed them a parcel of food and arranged to meet them the following day. They now returned to the workers' camp, where they had been perilously hiding at the mercy of any stool pigeon who wanted to curry favour with the Germans.

Over the next two days Grimson's assistant met them twice more and explained that George was on his way, probably accompanied by another escaper. At last, on the third night after their first encounter with the Pole, George arrived in person to their great relief and took them to a safe house in Gdynia.

George was not one to hang about; he pressed Gilbert and T-C to make their attempt the following night. They were as keen as he was, so as soon as it got dark, the three of them made their way to Danzig Docks and reconnoitred the hole in the fence used so successfully by Flockhart.

The Swedish ship, spotted earlier by George, was still moored close by, but a German sentry was guarding the approach to the gangway.

"Hang on a moment," whispered George. "I'll see if I can distract his attention, while you two nip up the gangway."

Before they could stop him, he had sauntered over to the guard and began to talk to him. Gilbert and T-C realised that George was putting himself at extreme risk, but there was no time to stop and they could only cross their fingers. Keeping as low as possible, T-C slipped through the hole, followed at an interval by Gilbert, and made for the ship.

Just as T-C hit the first rung of the gangway, the sentry spotted him. With a shout the German darted forward and grabbed him by the arm. Gilbert dropped flat and George withdrew a little. Protesting volubly but vainly, T-C was hauled off the ship by the sentry. While they were arguing on the quayside, George signalled to Gilbert to board the ship. Jackie made a desperate break for it, scuttled up the gangway and dived into the bowels of the vessel. The guard, still exchanging words with T-C on the quay, was quite oblivious.

Jackie Gilbert remained quietly stowed away in a locker until the ship reached neutral waters. Eventually he made his way back to England via Sweden to win the Military Medal for his magnificent effort. Townsend-Coles, however, was arrested.

Any ordinary man in George's position would have made himself very scarce, but George Grimson did not leave a comrade in the soup. In the hope of creating a diversion which might give T-C a chance of making a getaway, he first mingled with the crowd which had gathered to watch the arrest. Then he shadowed T-C and his captors first to the dock police station, then to the railway and even on to the same train to Insterburg, where T-C was finally locked up. After that, it is believed Grimson may have returned heavy-hearted to Danzig to wait for the next escaper.

But there was to be no next one. The Escape Committee, alarmed by Nat Leaman's capture and the discovery of most of his papers, despite the valiant attempt to burn them, had closed down on all activities for the time being. All escape equipment was hidden in readiness for the big searches which were bound to follow. The wireless set, the one piece of cheer left to a rather apprehensive camp, was the only item still operative. That 'canary' still continued to 'sing' every night with verbatim reports from the BBC news as well as from the American News Service to Europe.

Otherwise we were in deep trouble. Nat Leaman's capture and the discovery of various little 'fiddles' here and there among the guards, had fairly put the wind up the Germans. They now realised that they were up against a highly-organised escape system which had not only operated successfully, but had also infiltrated their own ranks.

A further misfortune was the Gestapo's discovery of Sommers' real Polish name. This had been found in the notebook of a partisan who had been killed while trying to sabotage a bridge. The jigsaw was piecing together in a way which promised a very unpleasant future for many, both British and German.

A shaken Commandant had Jimmy Deans and Mogg brought before him and launched into a long tirade, the gist of which was he felt that he had been 'betrayed'. Although he knew Deans spoke German, Mogg and many others pretended not to; but they understood the language perfectly, so in future the only language to be spoken in the camp would be German. The most unpleasant part of the interview however, was the Commandant's frequent, and possibly significant explosion of *"Deans und Mogg kopf ap!"* (heads off).

The Commandant also interviewed Nat Leaman, who immediately demanded the restoration of his Royal Air Force uniform, of which he had been deprived after he had refused to make a statement about what he was intending to do when he got away. That, he was told, was a matter exclusively for the security staff. But Nat was another unbeatable one. The following day he bluffed one of the German jailers to go over to the compound and fetch him his uniform. Behind the familiar blue tunic and brass buttons, he felt rather better "and just that teeny bit more secure", he observed later. Nat was interrogated daily at all times of the day and night, then suddenly released and put back into the compound. He had been through a nerve-shattering experience, but they got nothing out of him.

For a few days things were quiet, ominously so, except for one morning *Appell* attended by the Commandant in person accompanied by extra guards and officers. He stood erect while his English-speaking interpreter used English for the first time in days. His job was to announce the massacre of the escapers from the officers' camp at Sagan, "all shot while attempting to escape". If he expected to frighten any one he was mistaken. For a moment there was stunned silence. Then people began to realise that the men shot were only the ones recaptured and that there were more on the loose. Some would be sure to get back to England.

A small cheer broke out. It swelled into the customary three loud hurrahs which we always gave on the King's Birthday, come hell or high water.

The Germans were thunderstruck. What sort of men were these who could cheer at the death of their friends and close comrades? The Commandant rightly decided that it was defiance and stalked angrily off the parade ground to cries of "murdering bastards, we'll catch up with you all". He was a shaken man.

To this day I don't really understand why we cheered. It seemed the only thing to do. Cheers or tears? But what better way to speed those valiant souls than the cheers of their own Service.

There were some who believed that this was just a piece of typical Jerry bluff. But a few days later the midnight news contained the then Sir Anthony Eden's statement to the House confirming this horrid crime.

Chapter 14

THE lull in German pressure at Heydekrug was deceptive. The unravelling of our escape apparatus by the Germans was still gathering momentum. Through Munkert, the Escape Committee learned that intensive investigations were being pursued into the documents removed from the guardroom fire. When it was found that some of these included genuine photographs, the trail led straight to Sommers, who was the camp photographer. He was closely questioned, but as news of the Gestapo's suspicions of him had not yet come through, he was able to talk his way out of trouble for the time being.

Poor Munkert was under suspicion because of his association with Nat Leaman and other escapers. All the same, a message was got through to Munkert to urge George: "Get out of the country. Our position is hopeless." Whether or not George received that warning no one knows. It is possible that he was arrested at Insterburg not long after this, still trying to do something for Townsend-Coles, who was in fact already being brought back to Heydekrug.

Two days later the Gestapo caught up with Sommers. He was brought into the camp and the prisoners of the escapers' hut were paraded before him. He scrutinised everyone closely but did not pick anyone out. Then, at a propitious moment, he pulled up the leg of one of his trousers to reveal that there were no laces in his boots. It was stupid of the Germans to have allowed this, for each of the prisoners he was facing had been inside the cooler and knew that bootlaces, belts and braces were always taken away from its inmates. Sommers' quick thinking had made it plain to his British comrades that he was under arrest. Later he was confronted with Townsend-Coles in the camp gaol. Both denied knowing each other.

The Commandant now sent for Jimmy Deans again. Escape, he said to Jimmy, had clearly become highly dangerous: all existing copies of forged documents should therefore be surrendered. If that was done, he would report to higher authority that he had found all false papers and the whole matter would be closed. Failure to comply, on the other hand, would lead to untold trouble in the way of searches and arrests.

Who was going to believe that? Looking straight to the front, Jimmy Deans said he had no knowledge of any such forgeries, but would make enquiries when he returned to the compound. After a consultation with the Escape Committee, he returned to the Commandant and told him that there were no other forged documents in existence.

St George's Day, 23rd April 1944, brought tragedy. A note from Munkert was delivered by another collaborator. It revealed that the Gestapo had caught up with Sommers at last. They had now connected him with the name of the man in the dead Pole's notebook.

Sommers was only a youngster, but he had been in Gestapo hands before. In a note he said he just could not trust himself not to break down under the sort of interrogation he could expect. He was bound to be shot, but he would prefer to die without having vital information extracted from him. He therefore asked the Committee to provide him with the means of taking his own life. This was done.

Early next morning it was learned that Sommers had died during the night. A young Pole had laid down his life rather than put in jeopardy the lives of foreigners who had gone to war to help his people. This was the most heroic gesture of all. May it long be remembered by every Pole and Briton and may God have a special place for Sommers in Eternity.

Altogether it was a bad day. Soon after the Committee knew of Sommers' death, they heard that a guard who had helped find a safe house at the forester's for Grimson and Flockhart had been arrested at the same time. This man broke away from his escort in an attempt to get shot, but was recaptured uninjured. But even the most stringent interrogation gained little from him, for he had known nothing about the escape organisation in the camp and nothing of Grimson's movement once he had changed ground to Danzig.

Later information suggested that this man was only one of several Germans executed for their part in the Grimson route. The same day the alert ears of the intelligence organisation heard from other Germans that Munkert was in trouble, was being watched very closely and was practically under open arrest.

But now the Germans seemed to have adopted more sophisticated methods and it was clear that someone of higher-than-usual intelligence was directing the moves. A note was received from Munkert saying that he had been cleared of any charges and was again available. He asked for instructions for the meeting already arranged to take place between himself and Grimson later that week.

The Committee was in a quandary. Was this a trap or was it genuine? They were suspicious, but contact with Grimson was vital if he was still at liberty. They had little option but to send a letter to Munkert via the only German available, though in the past the latter had not proved particularly trustworthy. Such risks have to be taken in war.

The letter detailed the events of the past two weeks and ordered Grimson to leave for Sweden at once. It was not signed; but unfortunately an accompanying letter to George from a close friend *was*. No Germans were mentioned by name in either letter. The letters were made up in a package with one thousand Reichsmarks and handed to the German on 28th April.

The German emissary did not return to his normal place of work, the carpenters' shop in the *Vorlager*, that afternoon. The men waiting anxiously for news inside the compound now had a grim suspicion that they had been trapped.

That evening a ferret brought in news of Grimson's capture at Insterburg, where he had been allegedly posing as a civilian in the employ of the Luftwaffe. We did not believe him.

Munkert was arrested the same day by the Gestapo. The details of his capture are not known, except that he was executed after the most brutal interrogation. In requiem one must say of Adolf Munkert that he lived and died by his Christian standards. Like many other Germans of much higher rank and family, he gave his life in the fight against Hitler. He was an ordinary, little man; he might have appeared weak, but he was strong in his Faith.

Fifteen Germans who had been working with the escape organisation were arrested and an unknown number executed. All Poles and German civilians who had been seen to have anything to do with any of the prisoners disappeared and were never seen in the camp again. Rumour had it that they had all suffered the Gestapo's favourite treatment of *Nacht und Nebel* (night and fog); that meant arrest in the early morning darkness, a few minutes to gather belongings and dress and then disappearance into the unknown. For most of the Germans one could feel little compassion. Unlike Munkert, who had died for the things he believed in, they were simply avaricious soldiers ready to sell their country for a packet of cigarettes or a bar of chocolate. No sympathy was wasted upon them.

Next morning, 29th April, the *Abwehr* struck again. Six prisoners, including the one who had signed the letter to George Grimson, were suddenly arrested and lodged in the camp cooler. In their eagerness the *Abwehr* missed many of the key members of the escape organisation. Quite by accident, though, they picked up Willy Woods, an Ulsterman, who was an important operator in our top-secret undercover link with England and therefore had nothing to do with the Escape Committee at all. Twenty-four hours later, the remaining members of the Escape Committe learned that Townsend-Coles was being kept in the cooler, but was being allowed no communication with other prisoners.

The disturbing news that Townsend-Coles was still in civilian clothes was also gathered by intelligence. Warrant Officer Taylor-Gill, now managing the Escape Committee with his customary efficiency, and the rest of the escapers were worried that the Germans had an ulterior motive.

Townsend-Coles still had his prisoner of war identity disc, but that would be of little help to him if he appeared before a military court wearing the civilian clothes in which he had escaped. Attempts to send a uniform or buttons over to him were frustrated time and again.

One member of the Escape Committee who was also in the cooler managed to filter through the news that he had been able to snatch a brief word with Townsend-Coles. This was how we learned that Grimson had been a passenger in the same train wherein T-C, under guard, had travelled on from Marienburg to Heydekrug. Although T-C had glimpsed Grimson more than once, they had no opportunity to speak, because the guards took unusual care to keep Townsend-Coles segregated. T-C had last seen Grimson when the train had stopped at Insterburg; there he had disappeared. According to the guards a nationwide search for George had been mounted.

Townsend-Coles, still without his uniform, was taken out of the camp and moved to Tilsit Civil Prison on 6th May. After enquiries had been made by the British Government through the Protecting Power, the Germans subsequently stated that he had been court-martialled on a charge of espionage and collaboration with the Polish Underground. The statement concluded that at Tilsit he had shown resistance and had been shot dead.

The British Government rightly demanded an enquiry, but time was running out for the Germans. Before the diplomats had got around to implementing the request, the Russians had overrun the area and that ruled out further investigation of the case.

So passed Townsend-Coles, a brave and honourable man, who had struck more than one shrewd blow for his country. One can only hope that his killers were scooped up by the Russians, who were notoriously unkind to most Germans of that sort they captured. They too had suffered from the 'Third and Last'.

The six men who were arrested at the end of April were removed from the cooler under heavily-armed escort on 10th May. Nothing further was heard of them until much later, when it transpired that they had been split into two parties of three and had eventually arrived at other prison camps in Germany. Their journey had been horrific and obviously designed to break their spirit. At night they had been thrown into pig-sties, chicken-runs and the foulest possible places on the way.

"What made it worse," said Willy Woods afterwards, "was that while we were languishing with the pigs, the sentries would spend their time debating loudly how and when they would shoot us. The excuse, of course, would have been 'while trying to escape'."

This was near-torture, because they were all German speakers, as the guards knew very well.

"From one day to the next, we never knew whether we were going to get the chop or not," said Willy.

All the six were therefore pretty relieved, after many weeks of wandering in disgusting conditions, to find themselves back in normal prison camps. They were still regarded by the Germans as particularly dangerous, but they were at least with their own countrymen and under the care of the Protecting Power, though this protection became less powerful as Himmler took over control and Schickelgrüber went further round the bend.

Nothing certain was heard of George. There were rumours of him rowing around Danzig Harbour, joining the Polish Underground and inflicting various forms of nastiness upon the enemy. To the men in the camp, George was the very symbol of escape. It just did not seem possible that this dedicated Pimpernel could be in enemy hands. That was the view and it still persists.

In the meantime, the world was breaking apart around us. One cold day in June, Bristow doing a routine test on his radio receiver picked up a German announcement that the Fortress of Europe had been invaded by the British and Americans. Cyril Aynsley went on the set that lunchtime and took the wonderful news that the Allies were ashore and staying ashore. Of course we had been expecting it, but somehow it had seemed as though D-day would never come.

It was certainly better news than we had been having a few days previously. With all Europe holding its breath for the great attack which would bring freedom at last, we learned that 80,000 of our miners were on strike. We could not believe such action of our own countrymen. It was inconceivable that with millions of enslaved people looking to us to free them even a small section of Britons could jeopardise the war effort for selfish reasons. Ninety-nine-point-nine per cent of the prisoners were bluntly in favour of shooting the miners and their managers, because there are no bad troops without bad officers. Nevertheless Ken Griffiths, later to take holy orders and emigrate to Canada, was vociferous in defence of the strikers, for he was a man of the Valleys himself. He insisted that freedom of action was in fact one of the objectives we were fighting for and why George and others had put themselves at risk. Perhaps he was right, but a lot of us still find it hard to forget this one. I am sure that the men who stormed the beaches were not enthusiastic supporters of the miners, any more than I am today.

Only four people in the camp knew of the invasion – John Bristow, Jimmy Deans, Cyril Aynsley and Ron Mogg. It was essential from the security point of view that the news should not leak out prematurely. In the event, it was the Germans who came into the camp, going from hut to hut amid cheers, with the news that the Allies had landed. After that it was a simple and safe matter to send out the news team with the BBC version, once the hut occupants had been warned by Tally-Ho against making any wild demonstrations. Looking back, I suspect the Germans were almost as relieved as we were. Here at last was something positive. The whole of Europe seemed to give a gigantic sigh of relief.

Escape was still in the air, but caution was urged, especially in clandestine messages received from home. There was also a sinister rumour or two going around. What would happen when the Allies advanced into Germany? What might the maniac in the Bunker order? We had a feeling that he might well decide to 'bung us in the ovens'.

A safeguard obviously had to be found. Accordingly, arrangements were made to build a transmitter as well as a receiver. The essential piece of equipment for this project was a diode-triode valve and that could not be manufactured from 'gash'. There was one, however, in a gramophone amplifier kept in the camp theatre. As this was Red Cross property, it was supposed to be sancrosant and not to be used in any warlike effort. Thus far we had carefully respected this code, but when T-G's intelligence indicated that the Germans meant to remove this temptation from our midst something had to be done.

In no time at all, John Bristow had built an infernal machine. This consisted of an alarm clock which at a given time actuated an elastic spring-loaded mechanism. That drew a box of red-topped matches across a piece of abrasive paper, giving ignition. The whole thing was wrapped in oiled rags and other highly-combustible material. With this it was planned to burn off the end room of the theatre where the amplifier was kept, saving, it was hoped, the theatre from complete destruction. The valves and other pieces of use in the set were of course removed before the action was scheduled.

The fire burst with amazing suddenness. We woke to a real crackle of flames. The Germans rushed into the camp with fire equipment which had never been used before, and amid the usual Teutonic chorus of shouts and yells, the fire party formed up and capered about in what no doubt seemed to them a madly efficient way. One of the guards eventually struck a dramatic posture, pointing the hose nozzle at the seat of the blaze and after more shouts, whistles blew and the water was turned on. The barest trickle oozed from the hose. While this contretemps was frenetically sorted out, the entire theatre block burned down. The flames were eventually extinguished by the prisoners taking over themselves and forming a bucket-chain to the fire pool. This we did only because we were afraid the fire would spread to the cigarette store nearby, or even burn down the whole camp.

John Bristow got his valves and the set was made against an evil day when we might have to call for help. We could not know the comforting fact that a whole parachute unit was standing by to drop in on us if we were seriously threatened.

The day after the fire, Heinze and his horrid mates in the *Abwehr* searched disconsolately in the ruins. All they found was a burned-out amplifier and a pile of charred gramophone records. The title of the top one, still readable, was *I don't want to set the world on fire*. John Bristow loved his little joke.

Relations between the prisoners and the jailers were not exactly cordial, but little was said. Not even Heinze could prove anything. Over in the *Vorlager*, however, a rash of posters appeared warning the Germans about trading with the prisoners. The most popular one, I remember, was a cigarette on spindly legs running through the wire.

Grimson, Jock Alexander and the others had certainly left their mark. The new Escape Committee under Taylor-Gill was getting down to some serious work, influenced only by the daily news of Allied advances.

It soon became very clear that the camp would have to be on the move as the sound of gunfire to the east was getting louder and more frequent. The Jerries, too, were looking less and less happy with the course of events, despite frantic howls from the depths of the Berlin Bunker. Tally-Ho therefore began to prepare for the forced march from the camp which seemed imminent. Advice was given on what to carry, the number of pairs of socks likely to be required and so on. Our Australian, Jack White, showed us how to make a 'swag' or pack constructed from a folded blanket with one carrying strap, a towel and a small bag containing toilet gear and other immediate necessities hung on the front to give it balance. The appearance might have been most unmilitary, but the only thing better than this traditional carrier of the Australian tramp in the Outback that I've discovered was a rucksack. Even then a swag had certain advantages, one of which was the speed with which one could get out of it.

With the Russians so close, the Germans were beginning to lose the superb cohesion which had kept their services together so well in the past. Now they were distinctly worried. They seemed obsessed with the aim of getting as much distance as possible between themselves and the Russians.

All in all it was a pretty tense time. Rumours of George and his activities still filtered back to the camp. Whether he was alive or dead at this time, he was still an inspiration and guiding light.

The announcement of the move came with dramatic suddenness. In A *Lager* a Test Match was in progress and the Australians were busy digging themselves in on the hard, sandy wicket. It was the last over or so of the match and victory was almost within England's grasp. Suddenly one of the German goons came in with orders for 'Dixie' Deans to report to the Commandant and for the camp administration to be ready to move.

'Dixie' Deans went off at once. The rest of us, since we had received no direct instructions, stayed watching the match. Each ball was bowled in a tense silence, each stroke and stratagem analysed and sometimes clapped. The quiet, decorous scene could have been Lords on a pleasant sunny afternoon, except for the wire and the thunder of guns away to the east.

'Dixie' was soon back and had his organisation quickly at work preparing the order of march. Some of the men, like Ronnie West and Gerry Tipping, were going to hide. They dug themselves out room under the Foodaco shop, tucked themselves away and hoped the Russians would soon overrun them. All were unlucky, however. As soon as the camp emptied, the *Abwehr* got busy with their trained dogs, which rapidly smelled out the prisoners in their hiding place. They joined us later.

The prisoners from three *Lager*, two British and one American, each of about the same strength, were split into two parties. Jimmy Deans' party had the best of it. They marched straight to Heydekrug station, where they were entrained under a strong guard. Jimmy had about 3,000 men under him and they faced an uncomfortable journey, as insufficient rolling stock had been assembled to do the job. Each truck was divided as usual into three compartments by barbed wire sections and forty hapless prisoners were packed into each of the end sections of a vehicle designed to hold just forty troops in total. Six Germans armed with automatic weapons and grenades occupied the middle section.

Slowly, with occasional stops to stretch tired and benumbed legs, the train made its way to Stalag 357 at Thorn in Poland. Amazingly, no one died of suffocation. When they first got out of the train at the new camp a week later, the weary, bedraggled men staggered like drunks, to the Germans' amusement. Eventually circulation was restored to cramped legs and we marched smartly into the new camp, already partly occupied by British Army captives. We were indescribably scruffy after travelling in the conditions already described and the waiting troops eyed us curiously, for our reputation had preceded us. But the Army was kind to us and we settled down quickly, although our new friends did not seem to share our feelings about escape. The general view seemed to be: "Why worry to escape? Our lads will be here in no time and by autumn we'll be back home in England getting ready to knock off the Nips."

Not long afterward the second party arrived – the two-thirds which had been split off from us. We thought that we had had a rough time, but they really had been ill-treated. After entraining at Heydekrug, this party of British and Americans arrived at Libau. There they were embarked on a small tramp steamer which would have only accommodated half the number in great discomfort. As it was, in sweltering July heat, they were packed into the holds and had the hatches battened down on them, except for the sick and wounded, who were left to lie on the open deck without shelter or care.

Altogether it was a brutal and rather hysterical business. Our Jerries were mainly concerned in getting away from the victorious Russians, leaving their own fighting men to mount a tremendous rearguard action, which even the British prisoners admired when they heard about it. There was no compassion or care for the many wounded, mostly Americans who had been shot down in the daylight raids and whose wounds were bound with paper bandages. Doctors Forest-Hay and Paddy Pollock performed prodigies of first aid when they were allowed to get near the injured.

The journey to Swinemunde lasted four days and three nights. During the trip a Russian aircraft appeared and made a half-hearted attempt to shoot up the ship. It was the first Russian plane the prisoners had seen or heard, although we were so near the East Front. The Red Air Force just did not seem to exist as far as we were concerned, despite what was said about them on the radio. Our own Air Force was in the sky every night and the Americans were busy throughout most of the daylight hours. The Germans who had invented the verb to 'Coventrate', were getting it back with interest.

On arrival at Swinemunde, the entire party, wounded and all, were crammed into cattle trucks and sent to Kiefheide, in Pomerania near Stettin. Here they detrained for their new camp at Gross Tychow, three miles from the station.

They were met by a posse of German guards with dogs. Some of them were German Navy, who claimed to have been sunk by British aircraft and machine gunned while in the water. Perhaps they had – both sides did such things; it happens in war. Anyway, they gave their prisoners absolute hell to make up for it.

The officer in charge of the guards behaved like a lunatic. These, he shouted in a frenzy, were the *Terrorflieger* who bombed German towns, killed their wives and children and destroyed their houses. He ordered the prisoners to march, then to run – even the wounded who were being helped along by their comrades. Vic Clarke, the *Lager* leader, tried to remonstrate with this madman and remind him that he was supposed to be a member of an honourable service. It was no use. The prisoners had to run, shedding many of the things they had carried from Heydekrug, and these were hurriedly snapped up by voracious bystanders.

Since everyone was heavily laden and completely spent by the journey, many prisoners fainted under the strain and fell. The guards at once attacked them with bayonets and rifle butts, while others incited the guard dogs to bite them. All the time the officer shouted and egged the guards on. The jabbing, biting and bayoneting continued until the last prisoner was inside the camp gates.

Chapter 15

A T Luft IV, Gross Tychow, 2,000 American NCOs were already in residence when our people arrived. More came later in the six weeks that elapsed before the Russians moved forward again and the camp had to be evacuated.

In spite of all that had happened, the nucleus of Grimson's escapers who were with the party still continued to preach the doctrine of resistance. Confusing the Jerry was still both a duty and a pastime, but escape was difficult because the whole area was in such a fluid condition.

Various members did get away, however, and reached places where they were overrun by Russians or partisans, who were to be found everywhere along the German lines of communication. One of these escapers, Warrant Officer Cyril Rolfe, contrived to get into a Russian POW working commando and then escaped from it. On his way east he met a Cossack raiding party and enrolled. In due course Cyril equipped himself with a horse, sabre and carbine. At one stage the brigade was surrounded by the Germans during a counter-attack. To extricate his men from the trap, the Russian commander ordered an attack and Cyril – who had never ridden before! – became the only known member of RAF aircrew to take part in a full-blooded cavalry charge. The breakout succeeded and a long time after joining the Red Army Cyril found his way home via the port of Odessa.

Meantime the party at Thorn had settled in. Their stay was to be short but well-remembered, for every Sunday a group of young Polish girls with short skirts and fine legs put on a gymnastic display on the road outside the camp. The Army was already used to it and pretty blasé; apart from that, they were older than we were. In some cases we had had nothing to do with women for years. It was no doubt a well-meant gesture by the Poles and certainly appreciated by the RAF prisoners – who, to quote one Army chap, "stood there with eyes like fried eggs".

The secret radio operated nightly, a performance which surprised the Army. The Tally-Ho organisation kept at it bringing in intelligence and preparing either to escape or to fight if it were necessary.

In spite of Army assertions that, as the RAF was the junior service, an Army NCO outranked his Air Force equivalent, Jimmy Deans managed to retain control of the camp. But it was a running sore which was never healed in the six weeks they spent at Thorn before another move put the issue on one side. All prisoners, Army and Air Force alike, were transported to Fallingbostel, 30 miles north of Hannover and uncomfortably close to Belsen.

When we arrived there were about 7,000 Army NCOs in the camp with no escape organisation or proper communications. Jimmy Deans set about reorganisation from Day One and an open clash of systems, threatened at Thorn, loomed closer. However proper organisation had to be achieved. Tally-Ho wanted to be active at once and hope of contact with George Grimson had not been abandoned. Such was the confidence each one of us had in him, we were sure that George would eventually send word and that we would be able to start up properly again. Moreover, the 1944–1945 winter was brutally bitter and Red Cross parcels were practically non-existent. Parcels from home, which were permitted every three months, failed to catch up with us. The parade ground and all the camp paths became a sea of mud and our boots rotted on our feet. Besides all this, there was a dreadful and palpable sense of disorganisation.

We realised that the first thing to do was to get Jimmy Deans elected Camp Leader. This was achieved at a mass meeting in which the political ingenuity of Peter Thomas played a large part. It was at this meeting that a famous Army remark was written into RAF history, when an Army Warrant Officer declared that "the Army has worked on seniority ever since the Battle of Hastings". After howls of laughter had died down, it was explained to the happy warrior that this was one of the few battles we had lost. In any case a large number of Army men were happy to vote for Jimmy Deans.

On his appointment, Jimmy formed a mixed administrative staff of Army and RAF personnel, notable among the former being Tom Cameron, Sergeant Major of the First Battalion, the Queen's Own Cameron Highlanders, who had fought to the last round at Tobruk; the Cameron Highlanders there had even been allowed to march past Rommel with bayonets fixed and pipes playing. From that time on, both sides worked together with incredible loyalty and friendship. The aim was clearly defined: the enemy was the one outside the wire. Of all Jimmy Deans' considerable achievements, this was probably the greatest.

In spite of the foul conditions in the camp, good fellowship was outstanding. When tuberculosis broke out, Doctors Forest-Hay and Paddy Pollock set aside one of the huts as an isolation hospital. Healthy prisoners from both services volunteered to care for their comrades stricken with the disease, although they knew there was little they could do for them.

Meantime the Red Army rolled steadily on to Warsaw, stopped on its outskirts and allowed the cream of Poland to be butchered by the Waffen SS. Night after night we heard of the Poles' incredible fight and of the failure of the Russians to help them. Only the RAF from a thousand miles away got through to the city to drop arms, ammunition and medical supplies. The 200 Polish airmen in our camp grew grimmer and grimmer, for many of them knew the Russians only too well. "We shall never be able to go home again," said one of them whose wife and child lived in Lwov, "the Russians are worse than the Germans."

Our little brush with the Warsaw rising was a poignant one. Some of the women and children prisoners were brought to our bath house to be de-loused after their long journey from Warsaw. The Germans forced the women to strip outside the bath hut before they went in for a shower to cleanse themselves, then made them stand naked outside while their clothes were cooked to kill the lice. An excited German rushed into the camp office to tell us about the 'peep show', which had been put on for our benefit. Jimmy Deans immediately called for his news readers, explained the situation and sent out orders that no one was to approach the perimeter of the camp where the Polish women were exposed to public gaze. Most people stayed in their huts or at the other end of the camp.

One of the decent Germans, however, got in touch with a Polish member of the RAF and passed over a message of appreciation from the leader of the Polish women. He also brought a request for any spare underclothes, shirts or pieces of cloth we might have to spare. The response was tremendous and, short though we were of that sort of thing, we managed to get several truckloads through the gate to these brave fighters of Warsaw. They included a boy, incidentally, just ten years old who had been awarded the Polish VC, the Virtuti Militari, for crawling under six Tiger tanks and knocking them out with sticky bombs.

The BBC was happily pushing out bulletins to the effect that the Germans were reduced to pushing into the front line so-called 'stomach battalions', or formations of men all suffering from stomach ailments. Despite this, instead of a Merry Christmas, we got the news that the Germans had blasted their way through the 'impassable' Ardennes in a classic move to split the Allied armies. If some stout hearts quailed at that moment and wondered if the Germans were really fighting us off with their crutches, the mood towards escape changed.

Once again the active Grimson-Morris-Alexander school began to make strong headway under Taylor-Gill. Even after Monty and Patton had sealed off the Bulge and shoved the Germans back where they came from, escape still had its difficulties. Shortage of rations, which was reducing most people to that pot-bellied form of near-starvation known to us as Kartoffel Gut, militated against it. We were too weak for a long run and there were not sufficient crops in the ground yet to sustain us. All the same, plans were made should the opportunity present itself, although we were becoming increasingly aware that events were beginning to take charge.

There was an echo from escape route days and George Grimson when Nat Leaman was taken out of the camp to face a court martial. He duly appeared before a *Kriegsgerichtsrat* of the Party and of course was found guilty. After some evidence in which espionage was mentioned and then dropped, he was finally charged with using forged documents to the confusion of the German military and civilian authorities. It was evident from his sentence that the Germans had now got the wind up well and truly, since he was given only three months hard labour and then returned to the camp. The Germans did not allow him defence counsel and in the event he was defended by Jimmy Deans and Peter Thomas, a formidable combination. As things turned out, Nat never did his 'time'. He just stayed quietly in camp 357 because the whole of Hitler's Thousand Year Reich was falling to pieces under the strain of relentless attack from the ground and from the air.

In retrospect, our time at Fallingbostel had a certain dreamlike quality after the hard days of endeavour, peril and achievement at Heydekrug. No one in the camp even considered for a moment that George might be dead. Through our communication with England, we knew that Paddy Flockhart had got back. Later we learned that Jack Gilbert had also made it. Even with only two back, everything had been worth while. We had scored many minor victories over Jerry with innumerable break-outs and two major ones in achieving the seemingly impossible and getting two men home.

So for the present we concentrated on living and gathering up loose ends. As more and more prisoners poured in, this in itself was a job. Eventually many prisoners had to be housed in tents on the parade ground.

There were some proud moments too. We all knew, through 'The Canary', of the incredible fight at Arnhem and were at the wire to watch when the prisoners from this epic fight were marched along the road past our camp by Sergeant Major Bill Lord. He had all the swagger of a Guardsman on parade. They were carrying their wounded and their guards were a shambling, dishevelled lot, just about keeping pace with the steady Praetorian tread of the finest soldiers in the world. We did not cheer. We came instinctively to attention and Bill Lord, noticing our two medical officers standing with us, gave his party "eyes right" and snapped them a salute which would not have been out of place at Pirbright or Caterham.

This was the sort of show England could really put on. None of us would have missed seeing it. The impression on the Germans was incredible. Though they found it difficult to understand the RAF, they were completely at home with the soldierly qualities of Bill Lord, who was later to receive the military version of the Order of the British Empire for his efforts in a prison camp.

When Bill Lord entered his compound, he was faced with labours as titanic as 'Dixie's', although directed towards different objects. He found soldiers of many races who not only looked defeated, but felt defeated and were dirty and scruffy. They stole from their comrades and were deep in all conceivable rackets. There was little evident morale and the German guards were pretty well as bad.

Lord started by cleaning out the barracks allotted to his unit, seeing to his men and caring for the wounded. Then he got the British contingent running on proper Army lines – all in record time. After that he looked around for French, Belgians and others with patent soldierly qualities. Within a week he had them organised as well.

However, Bill Lord lacked one thing. He wanted a good interpreter. He must have had a thought that although the RAF were an awfully scruffy lot, they might have the odd brainy one who could talk that stupid German lingo. Such was his ascendancy over the Germans that he arranged an official visit to us at 357 to consult with Jimmy Deans.

Accordingly the splendidly upright figure of the Guardsman appeared at our gate escorted by two German soldiers who were doing their best to look smart and a German officer who had clearly taken some pains over his turn-out. We presented him with one of the best German linguists in the camp and I am sure that Joe will bear with me when I say that at that time his sartorial standards and hair-do were hardly regulation pattern. A keen member of Tally-Ho with a cover job in camp administration, Joe was the one who was usually blamed by the Germans when anything happened they did not like. This was no rare occurrence and Joe's main complaint in the glorious summer of 1943 was that the only sun-tan he was able to acquire was on his arms. He was a sun-worshipper who used to stick his hands out of the cooler window when he was incarcerated to get some sunshine. When this idiosyncrasy was carefully explained to the Germans, they sympathised and were in no way disturbed when they saw pairs of hands sticking out of the cooler windows. What they did not know was that many of the inmates had been taught to 'speak' in deaf and dumb alphabet by Norman Hennessey. Joe's sunbathing efforts were therefore able to keep us well informed on what was going on in the cooler. In return we sent them the latest home news.

Anyway Joe and Bill Lord took a long look at each other and decided they might make a go of it. They certainly did, and Joe took with him a great deal of the know-how drilled into the camp over the years by 'Dixie', Jock, Alan and George. Three weeks later duty brought Joe back to the camp – and what a Joe! His long hair was short, his side-cap was glued on the side of his head at the correct angle and his cap-badge and buttons blazed. Even his trousers were creased and you could see your face in his boots. To cap it all, he was wearing a belt and gaiters. And they were all scrubbed white. He marched up to the camp with a back like a ramrod and, although not a particularly tall type, managed actually to look down on some of his old comrades. "You scruffy looking lot of sods," he shouted, "it's about time you smartened yourselves up a bit round here!" We could only gape with amazement. He did condescend to drink a cup of acorn coffee with us while he discussed the business of the camp. Sergeant Major Lord was certainly a fast and thorough worker. We could have done with him earlier in our own camp.

The other outstanding feature of Fallingbostel was that we were in the main target area of Germany. Night after night, we watched cascades of target indicators fall over Hannover and Bremen, accompanied by the steady beat of aircraft engines, the thunder of bombs and the rumble of flak. The bombers always left tremendous fires behind them. After one raid over Hannover, the sky was as light as day because of the glaring fires beneath. It was an extraordinary sight.

By day we watched the vapour trails high above as Fortresses and Liberators, accompanied by long-range Mustang fighters, fought their gallant way through to distant targets. Our hearts and minds were up there in the battle. Occasionally, a Fort or a Lib would drop out of formation and our Americans would try to kid us it was a flak-ship dropping astern to draw off the fighters. Flak-ship or not, the loner usually got the chop and we would look anxiously for the white parachutes to blossom against the sky. Usually a few did – I believe that the official statistics for all of us who jumped from stricken aircraft were about one survivor in eight. Anyway, a few days later there would be new faces in the camp and we would share with them what we had, while our two doctors, now joined by a third, Captain Davenport of the Airborne, did their best to cope with the wounded. They were sent to us with the minimum of treatment, though this was understandable as at this time the Germans had more of their own casualties than they knew how to cope with.

Due to lack of communications in Germany, however, fewer people were passed on to us through Dulag Luft. This failure to receive transports from the Dulag brought about a temporary hiatus in our wireless communications with home, for back at HQ in England someone had suddenly decided to change the cipher. The last persons to hear of this were, of course, the people for whom the messages were intended. Good old Headquarters, like the Germans, was putting too much reliance in the system based on regular transference of captured personnel from Dulag Luft. Unfortunately for them that system was bust.

We spent worried weeks trying to decipher garbled instructions from home. The best brains in the camp – and they included Senior Wranglers and men with high mathematics degrees – covered acres of paper with hopeful deductions, but still the messages came out gobbledygook. Come to think of it, perhaps it was just as well, because if we had been able to break the cipher, the Jerries, with much more sophisticated methods, would have been able to do so too. Eventually, just about the time we got news back to England that we had no key to the new cipher, a new prisoner arrived with just what we wanted.

For a few days all was well. Then England, having received our urgent message, reverted to the original cipher. Back to Square One. "If you can't take a joke. . . ."

Our removal to the south without being able to re-establish direct contact with Grimson meant that for the time there was no hope of operating the escape route. Whatever fresh escapes we made now would obviously have to be opportunist rather than carefully planned. The best the organisation could do would be to ensure that the escaper was well briefed and had as much as possible in the way of escape gear.

But rumour persisted at Fallingbostel that George was still on the loose. If it were true, premature disclosure that he had escaped might be embarrassing. On the other hand, German security seemed to know far too much about him, so that it was quite possible he was in their hands – or, worse still, in the clutches of the Gestapo.

It was therefore decided to inform the enemy, the Protecting Power and the UK that No 631689 RAF Warrant Officer George Grimson had escaped from Stalag Luft VI. The official letter added that contact had been made with him on a number of subsequent occasions. The enemy and the Protecting Power were being officially informed of his escape, so that the Protecting Power could ensure that if he had been recaptured he would be treated correctly. There was no reply to this message.

Nevertheless we hoped for the best and concentrated on plans for the future. The British and Americans had crossed the Rhine and were fighting their way deep into Germany, while the Russians were rolling up to the Oder, engulfing East Prussia and our old camp at Heydekrug in the process.

Even now we had not given up hope for George. He seemed to us indestructible.

Chapter 16

OUR own side set up one brief excitement before we left Falling-bostel. One night we caught the drone of a low-flying Mosquito, looking for trouble in the bright moonlight. This lad circled the camp seven times and each time he flew low near us, there was silence as every airman pictured what was going on in the cockpit and every soldier feared the worst. Finally he dropped a bomb on the *Vorlager*, gave the sentry boxes a burst of cannon shell and machine gun fire and, in the words of Ron West, "peed off home at a rate of knots to have his bacon and eggs". Our interest in all this was distinctly lively as we were crammed ninety to a room and two hundred in a tent, and had no air raid trenches. One German, *Oberleutnant* Schultze, endeared himself to us that night. Like an earlier *Feldwebel* of the same name, he was a favourite of all the prisoners, since he was a wounded parachutist who had knocked out a number of Russian tanks and wore Germany's highest decoration for valour. It was a pity he was born on the wrong side, because he was certainly not a Nazi. His English was limited and to the point. "All politicians are the same," he would declare, "they stink." Except for Churchill, we agreed.

As the Mosquito banked round the camp he decided it was his duty, since the prisoners had no trenches, to share something of their danger and walk around their quarters. "After all," he pointed out to Mogg, who he had turned out of bed to accompany him, "I am ze *Lager Offizier*. If there is strawberry jam I must be here to help clean up." As the two of them walked between the rows of huts, watched by the prisoners inside, he cheer-fully assured them that "All is vell, Schultze ist here, alle in de best confusion."

But the night was really Arthur Sharple's. The bomb fell and in the ensuing silence this former Spitfire pilot from Lancashire put on his broadest Lancashire accent to announce: "Ee, if blud smells like manure, I'm wounded." Everyone of the two hundred men cramped into his room burst into laughter. Long after the intruder was well on his way home, Arthur's homely jest was passing from hut to hut, tent to tent and the whole camp was rocking with laughter. This was hardly one of those complicated English jokes you had to explain to your American friends; they got the point right away.

However, the German officer touring the camp, was baffled. "Vy are they laughing?" he asked Mogg in his rather fractured Anglo-German. *"Alle Englander Geistlichkrank."* All the way to the gate Mogg tried to explain. Finally the penny dropped, Schultze gave a roar of laughter, shook hands with Mogg, and smacked him on the back. "Zey are gut soldaten, I vish they were mine," he concluded, as he made his way off to the German quarters.

Apparently Schultze then spent half the night trying to explain this great English joke to his brother officers, but without much success. Apart from the vagaries of Teutonic humour, another reason may have been that one German had been killed in bed with his Latvian mistress, while several others were wounded and a lot severely frightened.

Schultze was still laughing when he came in to take next morning's parade. His *Appells* were always models of good behaviour. He never harassed any one and if he found one of his guards prodding a prisoner or being unpleasant in any way he gave him a good old-fashioned 'cigar to smoke'. But sometimes, because of his unorthodox English, parades would become a little bit of a strain.

On his approach, the WO in charge would call the parade to attention and then turn and salute Schultze. He would return the salute with a solemn face and a piece of English profanity he had probably learned the day before. Next he would salute the parade and roar: "Bloody good morning!" To his delight this would be received with "And a bloody good morning to you!", instead of the blast of rudery usually thrown at *Lager* Officers on such occasions.

"Darf ich rühren lassen?" would be the WO's next remark, to which Schultze would respond: "Of course, you silly old bugger, they must stand so to be counted!" Then, after the order had been obeyed and the counting begun, he would stroll up and down with the WO in charge. "Now we tell *Witzen* . . . dirty stories," he would exclaim. He took no interest in the numbers returned to him, but concentrated on trying to translate dirty German jokes into English or vice versa. We were left in no doubt of the utter lavatorial simplicity of German *Witzen*; by contrast the English stories were generally more subtle and invariably a good deal filthier.

Schultze was openly contemptuous of the officers and men on his own side, unless they bore the decorations or other marks of service in the field in the First War. These were his kin. God knows what the German behind the lines thought of him.

Eventually they sent Schultze to fight in the west. "I am going to desert to become an Englishman," he joked the night before he left. We heard later that he had been killed. I hope it was only a rumour.

The loud noises we could now hear all around us were underlining the news we were getting, to reinforce the belief that we would soon have to be on the move again. By now even the most ardent Nazis were getting the wind up. Orders were followed by counter-orders and the Prisoner of War Command seemed to be caught up in a major panic. We also heard suggestions over the Canary that we might be held as hostages or, worse still, marched off to one of those infamous ovens, of which the Germans themselves seemed so curiously ignorant. Even if they did not know, a macabre joke about 'bad boys going up the chimney' was circulating. It was hard to credit that anyone could live as close to Belsen as we did without having some idea.

Then we got a no escape order from London over the radio. "Stay put", we were told. All very well: but supposing Germans over the other side of the wire were scurrying round busily organising our removal? The Grimson intelligence net was still working full bore and we prepared for whatever might come.

Inside the camp, not outside, a table of departure was drawn up. This aimed roughly at columns of about a thousand, each under its group leader, its security chief (in case the Jerries turned nasty) and a general headquarters of about twenty British and American prisoners who were to march somewhere near the centre of this great army of the unarmed but very bloody-minded. Bristow and his radio were to travel with the headquarters unit; they eventually kept us in touch with England every night of the Exodus except one, when we had to bed down in a field; on this occasion, even the ingenious John Bristow could find no wires to tap for power.

Head of the security side, should it come to a scrap, was RSM Tom Cameron of the Cameron Highlanders. Our other head of security was 'Splash' Oliver, once the youngest CSM in the Irish Guards and later a parachutist of distinction. He was captured when he was dropped on Mount Etna miles from his target with his batman as his only companion; as the two ex-Guardsmen tried to fight their way to the proper landing ground, they managed to take on a large part of the Italian Army with fatal results for many of them.

So it came about that when the German Commandant had 'Dixie' over to tell him we would have to move, a Warrant Officer of the Royal Air Force was able to retort that we were prepared and the order of march was already known to everyone. It merely remained for the Germans to tell us our destinations and arrange food and billets. The Germans were duly impressed.

We set off at the end of March after a tremendous raid on Hannover. Like the children of Israel, we were guided by a cloud of smoke by day and a pillar of fire by night. The only difference was that we kept well away from our guiding symbol. Rather like the Israelites, we wandered rather than marched across the byways of the Lüneburg Heath, where Monty was shortly to accept the surrender of the Germans.

From our headquarters, Jimmy Deans kept contact with 'his' Kriegies by means of a worn-out old bicycle which had a large patch on one of the tyres – a patch so big, in fact, that it bumped him up and down. Whenever he approached a column, he was roundly cheered and greeted with a short burst of *Here comes the Galloping Major*. Wherever he went he was attended by a guard riding an equally aged bicycle. The German march headquarters was close to ours, so that constant contact was maintained between the columns.

The long columns became thoroughly intermingled with German refugees as time went on and it was not unusual to find British *Terrorflieger* helping old people or carrying young babies to give their mothers a rest. Officially this was frowned upon. In some villages, Nazi *Baumeister* inveighed against it. But as far as our headquarters was concerned, we were under the German command of *Hauptmann* Ruste, who had been smashed up in Rommel's army; he was a real soldier and not a two-penny-halfpenny pretence in a brown or black shirt.

As we zig-zagged across the Heath, the sound of battle encircled us. Hopefully expecting release, we slowed our march to a snail's pace and demanded frequent halts.

There was an expectant moment when we caught sight of a British Army scout car, but soon afterwards there was an explosion and three more new prisoners joined us. They had run into a road block. From what they said we seemed to be in a sort of pocket away from the main fighting, but it wouldn't be long now. In our long trek we had barely seen a real road, but kept to the dirt tracks through the forest – which was just as well, our new boys assured us.

Jimmy Deans in his journeyings from column to column had his moments too. One night he had been with a column some distance from headquarters and had decided to bed down with them in a barn, which was then chosen as a target by a night intruder Mosquito. Several bursts of cannon shell set the barn alight, but fortunately none of our people were hurt.

The sky was full of Allied aircraft and we hurried to paint yellow stripes on our packs. Usually the planes kept well away from us and it was pretty clear that Command had a good idea where the prisoners were moving. We also made up yellow panels which we laid on the ground if an air attack seemed imminent. If at this stage the Air Forces did not trouble us, they left plenty of signs of the havoc they were creating in a disintegrating Germany. Whenever we saw a railway line, it was littered with blasted locomotives and burned-out trucks. In one place there was even a dead horse, which had been shot between the shafts. We had a good horse-stew that night.

At another place one of the columns which contained most of our

Australians marched through a flock of sheep. There wasn't even a bleat as the sheep were snatched up, quickly despatched, skinned and jointed while still on the march. Of all our people, the Aussies seemed best able to look after themselves and live off the land. The rural population, too, were increasingly friendly and bartering of cigarettes for eggs or chicken was brisk. In spite of occasional showers of rain and a night spent in the open in one of them, our spirits were high.

Jimmy Deans had only one order and that was: "When you go through a village, smarten up, march at attention and hold your heads high. Show these bloody *Herrenvolk* just who has won the war."

Every night the news came through and every night the same orders from London far away: "Do not attempt to escape. You run the risk of being killed." No doubt to a man sitting in England, these were sensible instructions, but they had little meaning for most of us. Our escapers had been shot at many times and were unlikely to worry much about that. Besides, we were airmen and had joined to fly, not to march around like a lot of 'Pongoes'. So there were many who, at the end of the day, quietly slipped off the end of the column and made for the sounds of gunfire. They got home first.

We had some bizarre encounters with our men who had got involved with other columns. One was with 'Slug' Warren, whom we came upon dressed in the uniform of the French Foreign Legion with a party of captured Legionnaires. Before our columns separated, he assured us that George Grimson was still alive and well; he had heard this through a French network, he said.

We reached the Elbe at a place called Bleckede late in April and many of us took the chance to strip off and have our first all-over wash for months. The water was cold but stimulating – though not half so stimulating as the news that there was a barge full of Red Cross parcels at Bleckede in charge of three Frenchmen who were determined not to give any up to marching troops. They were speedily visited by Jimmy Deans accompanied by a party of armed Germans. After considerable argument and arm-waving the Frenchmen were persuaded to do their duty and form a Red Cross food dump for the prisoners passing that way.

With the aid of many volunteer work parties the barge was unloaded in record time. The Germans, who with the exception of the Nazis and Gestapo were incredibly honest, placed a guard over the dump while we superintended the issue to the other columns. No doubt most or all of the Germans accepted a gift of coffee, cigarettes or chocolate which we were glad to give them, because in our march we were all rapidly becoming part of the same outfit. Most of our guards were old or wounded men; we even had to carry their rifles for them.

A happy crowd of prisoners and guards crossed the Elbe by a ferry which consisted of a dumb-lighter lashed alongside a small motor boat. The river on the far side was manned by funny little men in chocolate-coloured uniforms who smelt of violet oil and sweat. We were told they were Hungarian infantry. We were not impressed.

When we were halfway across the river, there came a whistle and a bang, and then another, so that we landed hurriedly amid cries of "*Schnell!*" The soldiers among us soon spread the word that the gun was a 75 and was no doubt mounted on a British tank which had the river in sight. We argued with the Americans whether it was a British or American tank – as if at this stage it would matter which one of them blew us up! Shortly afterwards the little brown men passed us at the double and disappeared in a wave of violet-tainted air. We felt that liberation was close.

The following day came dreadful news. One of our columns, marching on a metalled road and carrying their Red Cross food boxes on their shoulders, were suddenly attacked by four Typhoons of the Second Tactical Air Force. We had nearly a hundred casualties, some thirty of whom were dead or dying. Worse still, they included some of the old hands who had stuck it out since they were captured in the battle of France and had spent their time digging tunnels and trying to escape. They had been tragically mown down almost in sight of freedom. It was a shattering blow, mitigated only by outstanding examples of individual bravery in rescuing and giving help to wounded men while still under fire. Of the many people one could mention in this instance, there is one outstanding example – our Non-Conformist minister from the Channel Isles. A civilian who had been attached to us contrary to the Geneva Convention, he was worth his weight in gold and an example to us all, in or out of uniform.

A white-faced Jimmy Deans heard the news and visited the scene of carnage at once. As soon as the dead had been buried and the sick put into hospital, he presented himself to the Commandant, who had lost twelve of his own guards in the attack.

"I must be allowed to go through the German and British lines and put a stop to this sort of thing," he told the Commandant. "I will take Charlie (his guard and interpreter) with me and I give my word of honour to return."

While the rest of the column marched north, deeper into Mecklenburg – but being careful to keep into what the Germans considered was the area to be occupied by the British – Jimmy and Charlie made their way to the battle lines armed with a safe conduct signed by the Commandant. Had they met Nazi or SS troops they could have been shot or hanged, but they encountered only regular units of the German Army and were smoothly passed on through their fighting formations until they reached no-man's-land. This they crossed, still on their bicycles, to be quickly picked up and taken to a forward Allied brigade headquarters. Jimmy's message was then passed smartly to Air Command, where there must have been considerable coming and going. They then settled down for a good night's rest, their first for a long time,

Next morning Jimmy Deans, accompanied by Charlie, went to get his battered bicycle to return. "Surely you can stay with us?" exclaimed an astonished Brigadier, "it's only a matter of days and meantime this German (Charlie) can go to the cage. He'll be well looked after."

"My escort is not a prisoner, sir," explained Jimmy. "He volunteered to come with me and I have given my word of honour to return to the Commandant."

"There's not much we can do about that then," said the Brigadier. "I admire you for it – but I'll certainly send you both back in better style than you came here."

Accordingly a jeep carrying a Red Cross flag took them to the nearest German-held post and the position was explained. Charlie confirmed to the German captain in charge that the story was true. This was completely acceptable to the German Army code of honour and a German vehicle was found to take them to the prison Commandant. Behind them the sharp sounds of battle then re-started.

But the Brigadier was right. It was only a few days later, 2nd May, that Montgomery took the surrender of the German forces opposed to him. By that time, a fighting patrol of the Queen's commanded by Lieutenant Potts had reached us and the Germans were marching back down the road to prison camp.

I watched them as they were lined up and pushed into place by a tough sergeant who had passed through the horror of Belsen only a few weeks back. Suddenly I did not feel like watching or cheering any more and I walked up the road with Cyril Aynsley.

"I must be a sissy," I confided to Cyril. "I know they are a lot of bastards and I hate their guts, but I just can't stand watching all that. It's a bit too close to home."

"If it gives you any comfort," grunted Cyril, "that's just the way I feel."

Epilogue

AFTER it was all over and I was sitting at a Whitehall desk in the special department set up by the Air Ministry to deal with NCOs' prison camps, it all seemed a very long way away. Most of them had been overrun by the Russians. Ex-prison guards as well as ex-Nazis and ex-Gestapo men were hard to find by our Search Teams, even if they were still alive after the Russian forward troops and partisans had passed by on their way to Berlin.

The mystery of George Grimson's fate has to be seen against this background.

On release, most RAF prisoner formations fragmented as characteristic individualism and a strong desire to make tracks for home asserted themselves. Some portable food and drink, a car, petrol and a Lüger or submachine gun – these were the first targets and easily 'acquired' by men who had spent several years of robbing their captors in the line of duty. Besides, many German units were being disarmed in the area and Kriegies wanted for nothing among the sympathetic fighting men of our own armies who had captured them.

Soon scores of prisoners in car-loads of three and four were speeding west, all bound for the Channel ports, the sea and home. Many failed to make it in one. Allied back-area troops, unlike the fighting men, seemed anxious to put ex-prisoners of war back in 'suitable camps for repatriation'; others were glad to get their hands on a car or any stray 'loot'; while in the opinion of some Kriegies, a proportion of the MilGov characters well behind the lines could have taught the Gestapo quite a bit had they been around to learn it.

We made our way back in a 'borrowed' Horsch shooting brake. As we walked into the collecting centre, we encountered an anxious Jimmy Deans and an equally worried Wing Commander Bill Jennens, an old friend and an escaper of note in the officers' compound from early days.

"We thought you'd been knocked off," explained Bill over a champagne. "Not everyone of the old gang is getting through OK. Some of the bastards are having their last fling."

"Is there any news of George yet?" we asked.

"No nothing definite. We are picking up bits of information here and there, but it doesn't look too good," said Jimmy.

We decided we might as well celebrate and drink to absent friends in any case. There was a great deal of sherry available, brought across from the captured bodegas in Bremen, so we had a party. For myself, it was a whole year before I could face sherry wine again!

We retrieved our car next day after a fight with MilGov and others. Most of the contents had disappeared, but we had our car and made our way to Brussels. There, walking smartly along the road, was an Australian we recognised at once in spite of his immaculate officer's uniform. It was our old friend Godfrey.

"You'd better get rid of that car," were his first words after picking him up. "If you don't those MilGov bastards will be on you like a ton of bricks. Bad as the Germans they are. Take me into town and I'll get you something for it."

This was duly done and we later spent the money re-kitting ourselves at the Officers' Shop as Godfrey had done – although we did not have the neck to commission ourselves.

Godfrey let it be known that there were many ex-Kriegies living it up in style in Brussels and some had even managed to get in a holiday on the Riviera.

"I've got a cobber in a Lanc squadron," he confided. "He'll take you anytime you like and bring you back here."

We declined the offer. Carrying the two secret radios as we had been instructed to do by someone in Britain on the day after we were liberated, we duly reported ourselves by taxi at the old cavalry barracks which had been taken over by the RAF. They seemed extraordinarily pleased to see us, although the constant squirting with DDT – "Hold the front of your trousers out as well, please" – did become a little tiresome.

But we were given a great welcome in the Mess and allowed to demonstrate our radios. In fact it was on one of them that we listened to Churchill's declaration of the end of the war against Germany. Ron Mogg, who took the news, confessed afterwards: "I had the wind up properly, there were so many people in the room. It was the first time in years since I'd taken the news down without being dead scared that the Germans would catch me and knock me off." Taking the BBC news or listening to Churchill was a terrible crime in the eyes of the 'Third and Last'. Like so many other little things, it was punishable by death or concentration camp, which was usually the same thing.

It took people a long time to become normal after living in Hitler's Germany. At Brussels there were more interrogations. Gradually our friends began to be accounted for: Alan Morris, Jock Alexander, Nat Leaman and Billy Woods. But still no George Grimson. We were beginning to get worried.

In England there was a quick trip from the reception centre for further interrogations. Then I was granted four days' leave before returning to the special department of the Air Ministry which was dealing with our camp. We know now that most of the men who killed our officers after the great escape were eventually punished, but nothing much has been said about those involved in the murder of Townsend-Coles. One can be pretty sure, since the Russians overran the area, that they did not escape. In any case there were plenty of Poles around to dish out some rough justice.

But we were not particularly worried about revenge. We were concerned to find George or at least to establish how, where and when he died.

After three years of investigation, the Air Ministry certified his death officially. On the death certificate, issued in London on 25th March 1948, it is stated that "according to the records of this Department 631689 Warrant Officer George John William Grimson, Royal Air Force, who was a prisoner of war in Germany, is presumed for official purposes, to have lost his life on the fourteenth day of April 1944". Just that and nothing more.

I feel bound to say that having weighed the evidence, and after so many years without further information, I am inclined to believe that the official conclusion is the right one. Many others do not believe it. The boy from Putney had created a legend of indestructibility. His strange wandering spirit, his aloof high-mindedness, could have found so many new altars upon which to lay his unique devotion. There was nothing inherently strange in a sudden or prolonged disappearance.

Then again the evidence, such as it is, may suggest death, but is far from conclusive. Judge for yourself.

George's brother John had been informed officially that Grimson was posted as 'Missing'. Many of us – Jimmy Deans, Cyril Aynsley and Nat Leaman besides John – continued to press for action, although most of us were back in our civilian jobs by then. It was not until 6th February 1946, that John was asked to "accept the Department's sincere apologies" for omitting to mention in their letter of a month earlier that it had been necessary to reclassify George as "Missing while prisoner of war, with effect from 1st December, 1945".

That was something, at least. The letter went on to assure John Grimson and his family that enquiries were still proceeding; should any news be forthcoming they would be notified with the least possible delay.

In fact, a great deal was happening in the search for George. His old comrades, especially Paddy Flockhart, were remorselessly turning out the facts, though they were not getting spectacular help from the Russians; not unnaturally after the pounding they had received, they were too busy taking it out of the Germans.

More official news came from the Air Ministry's casualty branch on 15th March 1947. John Grimson was told that they wished "to explain that enquiries are still proceeding in the hope that reliable information concerning your brother's fate may be elicited". A sinister beginning to a letter which became more sinister as it proceeded.

"The Department," it continued, "is sincerely anxious that this information should be forthcoming, for unhappily, in view of the time that has elapsed since your brother was last reported alive, it is evident that his death must be presumed to have occurred.

"You will appreciate that great care must be taken in determining the true date of his death, not only because subsequent information eventuating may render a perfunctorily assessed date invalid, but because it will influence the extent of his service estate.

"At the moment the Department is in possession of two conflicting reports, neither of which has been authenticated, and which show a discrepancy of a year in the relevant dates. In one case your brother is said to have been shot in April 1944, while the other implies that he may have been alive in April 1945.

"You are assured that this Department is by no means unmindful of your mother's predicament. The hope remains that the Search Bureau in Germany may yet obtain the particulars that are so urgently sought, when a letter conveying the substance of the report rendered, together with the required certificate of death, will be forwarded at the earliest moment possible." A sad predicament for the civil servants, particularly the pay branch who were evidently not 'unmindful' that they might have to fork out another year's pay.

What then were the conflicting reports? In fact there were more than two.

Alan Morris's was one of the most puzzling: "In January 1944, W/O Grimson left Stalag Luft VI to go underground. It is believed that he was captured early in April 1944, by the Gestapo at Insterburg railway station. This information quickly found its way back to Stalag Luft VI and I have no reason to doubt its accuracy.

"I was then removed to Stalag Luft III (Sagan), where I remained until the end of January 1945, when we were marched to Stalag IIIa.

"At Stalag IIIa there was a German, Major Goldt, in charge of American infantry prisoners. Major Goldt was a decent sort of man and a patriot. He would find out what he could for me in a general sort of way, but was not ready to give details of military importance.

"Major Goldt told me in mid-February 1945, that Grimson was all right, meaning I presume that he was in captivity but still alive and well."

Alan Morris added that he believed that Major Goldt had obtained his information from *Oberst* von Horman, who was also at Stalag IIIa and had been at Luft VI during the Grimson break-out and subsequent troubles of a year before. Alan was not able to confirm the information with von Horman, who had reached the age of 65 and was retired to civilian life.

"But," concluded Alan Morris, "at about 20th April 1945, Major Goldt told me that he thought Grimson was dead.

"A few days later Major Goldt and all the other Germans fled to the woods and on 22nd April 1945, the camp was liberated by Russian troops."

Jimmy Deans' official statement merely said that George Grimson was rumoured to have been arrested at Insterburg about 18th April 1944. He did not know where the rumour originated, but thought that it came from a German source.

Some members of the Escape Committee, the Search Team recorded, had picked up a rumour during the march from Gross Tychow to Fallingbostel to the effect that about August 1944, they had received a note from a French prisoner (name unknown) to the effect that Grimson was safe.

Warrant Officer Vic Clarke, who had commanded one of the compounds at Heydekrug under Jimmy Deans and had been the British Leader at Gross Tychow, was also interviewed, but was unable to give any new information concerning George's fate.

Corporal H. L. Barber offered some information of the last hours of George in the Camp, but nothing afterwards. He was the last of our men to see George before he made his escape and was at that time i/c RAF Intelligence Section in K *Lager*.

"I talked over the escape plan with Grimson who at this time appeared to be suffering from nervous strain," he records. "He fully appreciated the difficulties of the job he intended to do and told me that, if he should be arrested by the Germans after leaving the camp, his life would undoubtedly be in danger.

"He gave me to understand that he was carrying a loaded revolver and would use it rather than suffer recapture. He was a man of strong will and great courage and I have no doubt that he would put these sentiments into action if the necessity arose. From several remarks that Grimson made to me I believe he foresaw his own death and asked for my prayers on his behalf. This was the last thing he said to me."

Corporal Barber, who was in charge of one of the parties on the march from Gross Tychow to Fallingbostel, said that he had had no further word of George nor news of any message being passed to any member of his party.

W/O T. Maxwell, on the march from Fallingbostel towards Lübeck, records that on 21st April 1945, he met a Frenchman. "This Frenchman was wearing civilian clothes," he said. "He gave me the following message: 'I am alive and well and still in this country. Grimson'."

On the other hand, W/O B. A. A. Fowler made the following report to Air Intelligence: "At Stalag 357 in March 1945, one of the German guards (name forgotten), a former Communist, and very reliable, informed me that he had formed part of the escort when W/O Grimson, a Pole and a German were shot about April 1944. This guard had been at Stalag Luft VI. He used to trade with us and had known Grimson well." The guard does not appear to have told anyone else and investigations by the Search Teams failed to locate him.

During the march from Stalag Luft VI to Stalag 357, W/O F. S. Staley told of some Americans he met. "They said that they had encountered a Frenchman who asked if they knew Grimson," he recalled. "They said that they did not know him, because they were not from Heydekrug, but would pass on any message. The Frenchman said that Grimson was well and had asked them to pass on this information." This incident was supposed to have taken place about 1st April 1945.

No wonder the Air Ministry was puzzled. There were many such stories.

Two more rumours were picked up by a New Zealander, Sergeant J. D. Murray. One was to the effect that George had been caught by the Jerries and shot as a spy. The other – and many of his old comrades still for some reason or another give credence to this – was that George had been working with the Red Army advance forces at a place and time unknown.

W/O Nat Leaman recounted that while he was in the cooler after his own abortive attempt to escape, Townsend-Coles told him that George had tried to effect a rescue of T-C, when he was caught at the Danzig Customs House. When taken under escort to Tilsit or Königsburg, he saw George hopping in and out of carriages to keep up with him. He was told by two German NCOs from Heydekrug that George was on the Gestapo wanted list, that a dragnet was out for him and that he would soon be caught. Nat knew nothing more except for the many rumours circulating among his comrades. Later he heard one extra piece of information, that Mr John Grimson and his wife had received a letter from a prisoner of war written in French and asking for parcels. The address was Adjt. Chef Reginald Greyshon, p.w. number 1559, Stalag XIIIb, Widen-Oberfaltz. This clue, like so many others, was followed up by the Search Team and came to nothing.

Most of the above is noticed in the Search Team's report. They added: "You might like to know that all prisoners of war are loud in their praise and all refer to Grimson as the greatest man who ever lived."

No prisoner of war is likely to contradict that statement. Wherever he is, alive or dead, Grimson will remain a name never to be forgotten when ex-prisoners of war from the RAF foregather. They meet in many parts of the world still – in Canada, Australia, America, South Africa, New Zealand, Europe and throughout Britain. He achieved a victory over the enemy as tangible as any fought on the battlefield and one which was of significance and value to his country. He remains an inspiration to all who knew him.

It seems fitting in conclusion to quote the words of Jock Alexander, written in a report he made on Grimson's doings shortly after the war, because they seem to characterise the Grimson story:

"It may seem a bit dramatic and highly coloured. I regret that I cannot recall these things without some emotion. There is, however, no exaggeration and not a tenth of the real drama."